Understanding and Using AI

Understanding and Using AI

A Resource for Nonprofit Leaders

Daniel O. Livvarcin and Yacouba Traoré

BEP

BUSINESS EXPERT PRESS

Leader in applied, concise business books

Understanding and Using AI: A Resource for Nonprofit Leaders

Cover design by Daniel O. Livvarcin

Interior design by Exeter Premedia Services Private Ltd., Chennai, India

First published in 2012 by
Business Expert Press, LLC
222 East 46th Street, New York, NY 10017
www.businessexpertpress.com

ISBN-13: 978-1-63742-738-5 (paperback)
ISBN-13: 978-1-63742-739-2 (e-book)

Business Expert Press Human Resource Management and
Organizational Behavior Collection

First edition: 2024

10 9 8 7 6 5 4 3 2 1

Description

Embrace the future with confidence and harness the transformative power of artificial intelligence (AI) to supercharge your nonprofit's efficiency and impact.

Guided by our motto **"Don't be afraid, be prepared,"** this book demystifies AI, making it accessible and practical for everyday use in your organization. It provides straightforward strategies and real-world examples to show how AI can streamline operations, enhance your mission's impact, and revolutionize problem-solving.

This guide is your key to navigating the evolving landscape of nonprofit management, arming you with the tools and knowledge needed to thrive in an era of innovation. Prepare to lead your organization toward a successful, impactful future.

Contents

Testimonials

"This book stands out for its practical focus on AI, featuring pioneering models from Vectors Group that ensure sound technology integration and strategic alignment with an organization's mission."—**Solange Tuyishime, President & CEO of Elevate International**

"An essential guide for any nonprofit leader, this book demystifies AI, showing how it can fundamentally transform operations and magnify impact. Daniel and Yacouba have done a fantastic job. A must-read for the forward-thinking executive."—**Mustafa Zeki Ugurlu, President and Executive Director, World Veterans**

"This book is an invaluable resource for leaders navigating AI's transformative potential in nonprofits, offering effective strategies for those challenged to maximize impact with limited resources."—**Deirdre Freiheit, Sr. Leadership & Executive Coach/Former Non-Profit CEO**

Introduction

In the tapestry of human history, dreams have been the threads that weave our future. Each epoch, from the Stone Age to the modern era, has been shaped not just by what humanity could achieve but by what it dared to imagine. Yet, some dreams are so audacious, so beyond the realm of current understanding, that they couldn't even be conjured up in the minds of our ancestors.

Consider a person from the Stone Age, their daily life entrenched in survival and the tangible world around them. The very notion of human flight, of soaring above the clouds like the birds they so revered, would have been an inconceivable dream. Fast forward to just a century ago, when the idea of connecting with someone on the other side of the globe in real time, seeing their expressions, and hearing their voice as if in the same room, would have seemed like an impossible fantasy.

Now, we stand on the cusp of a new frontier with AI. What we are achieving with AI today was once a partially resolved dream, lingering on the edge of our collective imagination. Yet, even as we marvel at AI's capabilities—its ability to learn, to adapt, to enhance our daily lives—we recognize that we are merely scratching the surface. There are countless possibilities and applications of AI that we have yet to dream up, innovations that future generations may look back on with the same awe that we now reserve for flight and instant global communication.

In this era of rapid technological advancement, it's natural to feel a mix of excitement and trepidation. The future is unwritten, filled with dreams yet to be dreamed and realities yet to be realized. But our message is one of preparedness, not fear. "Don't be afraid, be prepared" is not just a motto; it's a guiding principle. It's a call to embrace the unknown with the knowledge that, just as our ancestors navigated the uncharted waters of their time, we too can face the future with confidence and a readiness to turn the unimaginable dreams of today into the groundbreaking realities of tomorrow.

In crafting this book, we've harnessed the power of AI to refine our content, ensuring clarity and precision in our message. AI has been instrumental in conducting fine-tuning and grammatical checks throughout the text, helping us maintain a high standard of readability and accuracy. Moreover, the engaging cartoons that grace the beginning of each chapter, designed to visually capture and complement the key themes, are the products of AI's creative capabilities. These illustrations, generated through AI, not only add an element of visual appeal but also reinforce the concepts discussed, making the material more accessible and engaging for our readers. Through these applications, we demonstrate the very essence of this book: showcasing how AI can be a valuable asset in enhancing the quality and impact of our work in the nonprofit sector.

Who Is This Book for

Over my lifetime, which is a bit over 50 years, I've seen a ton of tech changes that have really changed how we all live. Think about how we went from black and white TVs to colorful screens, then jumped onto the Internet, got hooked on social media, and now we all have smartphones in our pockets. Each of these changes was huge, shaking up our everyday life. But now, we're at the start of something even bigger—AI. It's more than just a small step forward; it's like a massive jump. AI is changing everything, from the way we do things to how we think about the world. It's making us rethink what's possible, with machines that can help us out and even spark new ideas for tackling big challenges.

This book is all about how amazing AI is, especially for people running nonprofits. We're inviting all the leaders out there to see what AI can do and how they can use it to do even more good work. We're not just watching this new age unfold; we're right in the middle of it, helping to shape it.

Welcome to a journey that bridges the realms of AI and nonprofit work. This book is crafted not for software engineers or mathematicians delving into the intricate technicalities of AI but for you, the nonprofit professionals, who are keen on exploring how this revolutionary technology can be harnessed to further your mission.

In the nonprofit sector, where resources are precious and the drive to make a meaningful impact is paramount, AI emerges as a powerful ally. It's a tool that can amplify your efforts, refine your strategies, and deepen your understanding of the communities you serve. This book aims to demystify AI, presenting it not as a distant, complex technology but as a practical, accessible asset that can transform your work.

We'll embark on a clear, jargon-free exploration of how AI can streamline operations, enhance decision making, personalize donor engagement, and measure the impact of your initiatives. Each chapter is designed to build your understanding and confidence in leveraging AI, with real-world examples, practical tips, and actionable insights tailored for the nonprofit context.

Our goal is to empower you with the knowledge to not just understand the potential of AI but to actively implement and benefit from it. Whether you're looking to optimize your processes, engage with your community more effectively, or unlock new insights from your data, this book will serve as your guide, showing you how AI can be an integral part of your mission to drive positive change.

So, let's begin this exciting journey together, exploring how AI can become a vital part of your toolkit, helping you and your organization achieve more and create a greater impact in the world you're striving to improve.

The Scope of the Book

This book delves into the intricate ways AI can be woven into the fabric of nonprofit management, touching on aspects of governance, strategic planning, and operational efficiency. In the realm of governance, we explore how AI can assist board members and executives in making more informed decisions, enhancing transparency, and ensuring compliance with ever-evolving regulations and standards. The strategic facet of the book examines how AI can aid in crafting more effective mission-driven strategies, from resource allocation to program development and beyond, ensuring that every step taken is data-informed and aligned with the organization's core objectives.

On the operational side, we unpack the transformative power of AI in streamlining processes, from automating administrative tasks to optimizing service delivery, thereby freeing up valuable human resources to focus on high-impact activities and direct community engagement. Throughout these discussions, the book maintains a focus on the practical application of AI in the nonprofit sector, offering insights into how these tools can be implemented effectively to drive organizational success and amplify impact. By providing a comprehensive overview of AI's potential in governance, strategic planning, and operations, the book aims to equip nonprofit professionals with the knowledge and tools to harness this technology in their pursuit of a better world.

In this book, we also introduce several innovative models developed by our researchers at Vectors Group, not as the primary focus but as foundational platforms that enhance the application of AI in the nonprofit sector. These models, the product of meticulous research and practical experience, serve as effective frameworks through which AI can be more efficiently integrated into various aspects of nonprofit management.

While the core of our discussion is not centered on the models themselves, their presence in this narrative is crucial. They act as conduits through which the power of AI can be channeled, interpreted, and applied to meet the specific needs and challenges faced by nonprofit organizations. By leveraging these models, we can demonstrate how AI can be utilized in a structured, goal-oriented manner, ensuring that its adoption is not just technologically sound but also strategically aligned with the organization's mission and objectives.

Thus, while the book's primary aim is to elucidate the broad scope of AI's application in governance, strategic planning, and operational efficiency within nonprofits, the models from Vectors Group provide a practical backdrop. They help illustrate how AI can be tailored and implemented to drive meaningful change, offering readers a clear pathway to transform theoretical AI potential into concrete, impactful organizational practices.

In this book, our primary focus has been on the integration of AI within the governance, strategic, and operational facets of nonprofit management. While these areas are crucial for the foundational and systemic enhancement of nonprofit organizations, there exists another dynamic domain where AI holds tremendous potential: direct service delivery.

Direct service delivery in the nonprofit sector encompasses the frontline services and programs directly provided to beneficiaries, ranging from educational initiatives to health care services, and from environmental conservation efforts to humanitarian aid. The application of AI in this domain can revolutionize the way nonprofits interact with and serve their communities, offering more personalized, efficient, and impactful services.

However, the depth and breadth of AI's potential in direct service delivery are so extensive that it warrants a dedicated exploration beyond the scope of this book. The nuances of how AI can enhance personalized care, optimize resource allocation in real time, predict service needs, or automate complex case management processes, for instance, could fill volumes with case studies, frameworks, and methodologies tailored to various service sectors within the nonprofit realm.

While we touch upon the surface of AI's applicability in direct service delivery, we acknowledge that this is an area ripe for further exploration. It's a domain where AI can make a tangible difference in the lives of individuals and communities, driving the evolution of nonprofit services toward greater effectiveness and empathy. We envision future works that delve into this exciting frontier, offering nonprofit professionals a comprehensive guide to harnessing AI in their quest to serve and empower their communities more profoundly.

Understanding the Transformative Potential of AI

AI is not just a field of technological advancement; it is a landscape of transformational potential that is reshaping the fabric of how we live, work, and think. To fully appreciate AI's transformative power, it is essential to look beyond its technical capabilities and understand the profound impacts it has on various aspects of society and industry.

AI has the power to revolutionize industries, creating new business models and paradigms that were previously unimaginable. In health care, AI is transforming patient care through advanced diagnostics and personalized treatment plans. In the realm of finance, AI-driven algorithms are reshaping how we approach investing, risk assessment, and fraud detection. The transportation sector is being reimagined with the advent of autonomous vehicles, while in agriculture, AI aids in optimizing crop yields and resource management.

One of the most significant aspects of AI's transformative potential is its ability to enhance human capabilities. AI systems can process and analyze data at a scale and speed far beyond human capacity, providing insights and solutions to complex problems rapidly. This augmentation extends to various fields, from scientific research, where AI accelerates discovery and innovation, to creative industries, where it offers new tools for artists and designers.

The implications of AI extend beyond industry and commerce into the broader realms of society and economy. AI has the potential to drive significant social change, offering solutions to global challenges such as climate change, health care accessibility, and education. Economically, AI can contribute to increased productivity and efficiency, though it also presents challenges in terms of job displacement and the need for workforce reskilling.

Understanding AI's transformative potential also involves recognizing the ethical considerations and responsibilities that come with it. As AI systems become more integrated into critical aspects of life, issues around privacy, bias, and fairness become increasingly important. The development and deployment of AI must be guided by ethical principles to ensure that its transformative impact is positive and equitable.

The future shaped by AI is one that holds immense possibilities. It is a future where routine tasks are automated, allowing humans to focus on creative and complex problem-solving. It's a future where data-driven insights lead to more informed decisions in business, governance, and environmental stewardship. However, this future also requires careful navigation, balancing the benefits of AI with the need for ethical, responsible development and implementation.

The transformative potential of AI is vast and multifaceted. It encompasses not just technological advancements but also profound changes in how we approach challenges and opportunities in various domains of life. Understanding this potential is key to harnessing AI's benefits while navigating its challenges responsibly.

Don't Be Afraid Be Prepared

Elon Musk, renowned for his groundbreaking work in embracing and advancing new technologies, has indeed voiced concerns about AI. His apprehensions resonate with a broader public unease regarding AI, stemming largely from uncertainty about its potential impacts. This fear is often fueled by not knowing what to expect from AI, a technology that is rapidly evolving and has the potential to significantly alter various aspects of our lives and society.

Musk's concerns highlight a crucial aspect of AI—the need for careful and ethical development and implementation. AI, with its vast capabilities, poses questions about control, privacy, job displacement, and decision-making processes. The apprehension is not just about the technology itself but also about how it will be used, governed, and integrated into society.

The fear of the unknown with AI is similar to the apprehension that has accompanied many major technological advances in history. However, the key to addressing these fears lies in education, transparent development processes, robust ethical standards, and clear regulations. By understanding AI's capabilities and limitations, stakeholders from all sectors can engage in informed discussions about how to harness its potential responsibly.

For nonprofits and other organizations, this means approaching AI with a balanced perspective. While recognizing its transformative potential, it's equally important to acknowledge and address the ethical and societal implications. This involves not only staying informed about technological developments but also actively participating in conversations about the ethical use of AI.

In the ever-evolving landscape of the nonprofit sector, change is not just inevitable; it's a constant. With the advent of new technologies, shifting societal needs, and evolving funding landscapes, it's easy for nonprofit professionals to feel overwhelmed or apprehensive. However, the key to navigating these changes isn't in resisting them, but in being prepared for them.

The introduction of new technologies, particularly AI, is a prime example. AI might seem daunting with its complex algorithms and data processing capabilities, but it presents immense opportunities for nonprofits. From enhancing donor engagement to streamlining operations, the potential benefits are vast. The apprehension around AI often stems from a fear of the unknown or a concern about the ability to adapt to new systems. But remember, every technological advancement that is now commonplace, like computers or the Internet, was once a new frontier. The transition to embracing these tools wasn't without its challenges, but the organizations that adapted and learned how to leverage these technologies effectively were the ones that thrived.

Being prepared for such changes means investing time and resources in understanding new technologies, training staff, and exploring how these tools can enhance your organization's operations and impact. It's about staying informed, being open to experimentation, and learning from both successes and failures.

Similarly, changes in funding models and donor expectations require a proactive approach. The traditional models of fundraising and donor engagement are evolving, and nonprofits must adapt to remain relevant and effective. This might involve diversifying funding sources, exploring new fundraising platforms, or adopting more data-driven approaches to donor relationship management.

Moreover, societal needs and priorities are constantly shifting. Nonprofits must remain attuned to these changes to ensure that their programs and services continue to address the most pressing issues effectively. This requires ongoing community engagement, regular program evaluation, and a willingness to pivot strategies as needed.

In summary, being prepared is about embracing change as an opportunity for growth and innovation. It's about fostering a culture within your organization that is agile, forward-thinking, and resilient. Don't be afraid of the new challenges and changes that come your way. Instead, equip your organization with the knowledge, skills, and adaptability to meet these changes head-on. By being prepared, your nonprofit can continue to make a significant impact, regardless of what the future holds.

Become an AI Whisperer

Welcome to the beginning of an enlightening journey that will transform you into an AI whisperer. As you start delving into this book, you're embarking on a path to understand and harness the power of AI, especially in the context of nonprofit organizations. Think of an AI whisperer as someone who has a special knack for understanding AI—not in the sense of conversing with machines, but in grasping how AI can be a powerful tool in your work.

Throughout this book, we will explore the essentials of AI: what it is, how it operates, and the myriad ways it can be leveraged to enhance and simplify the processes within nonprofit organizations. You'll learn about AI's role in financial management, team building, communication, and fostering partnerships, among other areas.

As you progress through these pages, the concept of AI will become less of a mystery and more of a practical ally. You'll discover that AI, much like a highly capable assistant, can process vast amounts of data, identify trends, and assist in decision making, all under your guidance.

By the time you reach the end of this book, you'll have gained valuable insights into using AI smartly and responsibly. You'll be equipped to lead the way in integrating AI into your nonprofit's strategy, enhancing your organization's impact and efficiency. This book isn't just about learning concepts; it's about preparing you to confidently apply AI in real-world scenarios, making your organization more effective and ready for the future.

So, as you turn these pages, get ready to become an AI whisperer—someone who understands and utilizes AI to bring about positive changes and drive impactful work in the nonprofit sector. Let's begin this exciting journey together, toward a future where you're empowered by AI to make a significant difference.

CHAPTER 1

Why AI Is a Game Changer for Nonprofits

Some people call this artificial intelligence, but the reality is this technology will enhance us. So instead of artificial intelligence, I think we'll augment our intelligence. [1]

—**Ginni Rometty**

Once, as a young professional fresh in the field, I vividly remember the day a new computer was brought into my office. The air was thick with anticipation, a sense of stepping into a new era. A young officer, brimming with enthusiasm, was tasked with introducing us to this marvel of technology. I watched, captivated, as he detailed the myriad possibilities that this machine could bring to our work.

However, my supervisor, a figure of authority and experience, was less impressed. After the presentation, with a note of disdain in his voice, he remarked, "It's only one step better than the typewriter. Now we don't have to rewrite the whole page for a single mistake; we can just correct the part that's wrong." His words fell like a damp cloth over my ignited imagination.

I remember feeling a mix of shock and disappointment at his narrow perspective. Here was a tool that I believed had the potential to revolutionize our work, our entire way of operating, and yet, it was being reduced to a mere error-correcting device. While I couldn't pinpoint all the ways this technology would reshape our future, I was certain it was destined for far more than just minor conveniences.

This moment stayed with me as a powerful reminder of how easily new technologies can be underestimated by those accustomed to the old ways. It also strengthened my resolve to always look beyond the immediate, obvious utilities of new tools and to envision the broader possibilities they could unfold.

Fast forward to the present, and I see the same pattern unfolding with artificial intelligence (AI). Just like the computer in my early days, AI is often viewed through a lens that barely scratches the surface of its potential. Many see it as a tool for automating tasks, improving efficiency, or analyzing data—all of which are true, but AI's potential extends far beyond these.

AI, I believe, is set to redefine the way we work, interact, and solve problems, much like computers did. It's not just about the tasks AI can perform but about the doors it can open—new ways of thinking, unprecedented solutions to age-old problems, and the ability to harness a level of data analysis and decision making that was previously unthinkable.

My experience with the computer has taught me to embrace new technologies with an open mind and a broad vision. As I delve into the world of AI, I carry with me the same sense of wonder and belief in its potential to change the world, hopefully, without the constraints of narrow perceptions that once tried to limit the scope of what technology could do.

AI is quickly becoming a big part of our lives. In just a few years, it's likely that AI will be everywhere, doing all sorts of things we see and don't see. Think of how we use smartphones or computers today—that's how common AI will be very soon. And by the time you're reading this book, AI will have grown and changed even more. It's like watching a small plant grow into an enormous tree faster than expected. This quick growth of AI is changing how we live, work, and solve problems, opening up new and exciting possibilities for all of us.

Even the brightest minds behind AI and the AI systems themselves can't predict where this journey will lead us. It's like setting sail without knowing precisely where the currents will take us. Yet, one thing is clear: the rise of AI is inevitable; it's a wave that's already begun to reshape our world. In the face of such an unstoppable force, the best strategy we can adopt is to be prepared. Being prepared means understanding AI, adapting to its changes, and learning how to use it to our advantage. It's about being ready to ride the wave rather than being swept away. This readiness will help us navigate AI's uncertainties and harness its potential to create a better, more efficient, and more innovative future.

The Game Is Changing

AI has rapidly transitioned from a niche technological innovation to a ubiquitous presence, fundamentally altering every segment of our lives. In business, AI is revolutionizing how we approach everything from marketing strategies to supply chain logistics. Companies now use AI to analyze consumer behaviors, predict market trends, and personalize customer experiences, turning vast amounts of data into actionable insights. This transition is not just about efficiency; it's about redefining business models and creating new avenues for growth and innovation.

In health care, AI's impact is nothing short of transformative. From diagnosing diseases with precision to personalizing treatment plans, AI enables quicker, more accurate medical decisions. It's not just in diagnostics where AI makes its mark; it's also in patient care and management where AI-driven applications help monitor patient health and predict potential health risks. This level of personalization and prediction in health care was unimaginable just a decade ago.

The educational sector, too, is witnessing a paradigm shift thanks to AI. Customized learning experiences tailored to individual student needs are becoming the norm. AI tools analyze learning patterns, strengths, and weaknesses, offering educators a more personalized learning experience. Beyond the classroom, AI enhances educational administration, helping institutions manage data, streamline processes, and improve overall efficiency.

In our personal lives, AI has become an integral part of our daily routines. From voice assistants that help organize our day to AI-driven recommendations on streaming platforms, AI's subtle integration into our lives enhances convenience and personalization. It's not just about smart homes or gadgets; it's about how AI understands our preferences, habits, and needs and continuously adapts to improve our quality of life.

Moreover, AI's role in addressing critical global challenges is becoming increasingly evident. In environmental conservation, for instance, AI is being used to monitor climate change, track wildlife, and optimize energy use. These applications show AI's potential to advance technology and contribute to a sustainable future.

AI is not just a game changer; it's a paradigm shifter in every facet of life. Its rapid integration across various sectors illustrates its versatility and potential to drive significant change. As we continue to unlock new AI capabilities, its role in shaping our future becomes more pronounced, presenting both exciting possibilities and essential considerations for its ethical and responsible use.

Nonprofits Are Not Exempt

With the advent of AI, the nonprofit sector stands at the edge of a massive change that can help it bridge the resource gap that has plagued it for so long.

Like everything else, AI will significantly impact the nonprofit sector, too, offering its organizations opportunities they could never have imagined. This transformative technology is not just a tool for efficiency; it's a gateway to possibilities that extend far beyond the current scope of thinking.

The nonprofit sector operates as our backbone social infrastructure, offering a unique and compassionate approach to addressing community issues. The sector is driven by a collective desire to contribute to the greater good, and its organizations usually exemplify a selfless dedication to improving the well-being of our communities. The altruistic ethos at the core of their mission propels them to tackle a diverse range of societal challenges, from addressing poverty and hunger to promoting education and health care. This altruism acts as a guiding principle, motivating these organizations to create positive change by leveraging the power of community engagement.

While the sector has evolved with increased recognition of its importance and a growing understanding of effective philanthropy, many organizations still grapple with limited resources. The demand for services and interventions often surpasses available resources, hindering the expansive reach of nonprofit initiatives. This scarcity not only impacts the scale of projects but can also constrain the ability of nonprofits to invest in technological advancements, professional development, and innovative solutions that could enhance their impact. As the nonprofit sector matures, the need for sustained, diverse funding sources and strategic resource management becomes increasingly evident to overcome the perennial challenge of scarcity.

In this challenging environment, AI holds immense potential to be a smart partner for the nonprofit sector, addressing several challenges related to resource scarcity and enhancing overall organizational efficiency.

AI and its various applications hold a tremendous transformative power to empower the sector with new resources, processes, and ways that will enhance the efficiency and effectiveness of delivering on their mandate. The multiplier effect that these new tools will create for the sector would help leverage their limited capacity to effect positive change on a greater scale.

For nonprofits, AI's influence means exploring new frontiers in connecting with their communities, managing their operations, and maximizing their impact. With its unparalleled ability to analyze data, predict trends, and personalize interactions, AI is poised to reshape the landscape of the nonprofit sector in ways we are only beginning to understand. This is a journey into uncharted territory, where the potential for innovation and growth is boundless.

In the context of HR capacity limitations, AI can serve as a force multiplier by automating routine HR tasks, leaving HR professionals with more time to focus on strategic initiatives. AI algorithms can analyze employee data to identify trends related to job satisfaction, performance, and potential areas for improvement. This data-driven approach enables nonprofits to make informed decisions regarding talent management, leading to better retention strategies and more effective professional development programs.

Regarding program development and implementation, AI can be a game-changer. Machine learning algorithms can analyze vast amounts of data to identify patterns and insights that inform the design of effective programs. AI can assist in predicting potential challenges, optimizing resource allocation, and even recommending innovative solutions based on successful practices in similar contexts. Automation in program monitoring and evaluation can enhance the efficiency and accuracy of impact assessments, providing nonprofits with real-time data to adapt and improve their initiatives continuously.

In the realm of fund development, AI technologies offer nonprofits innovative tools to optimize their fundraising strategies. Machine learning algorithms can analyze donor data to identify patterns and preferences, enabling nonprofits to personalize their fundraising approaches. Predictive analytics can assist in forecasting potential donation amounts, allowing organizations to tailor their campaigns to specific donor segments. AI-powered chatbots and virtual assistants can enhance donor interactions by providing real-time information, addressing inquiries, and facilitating seamless donation processes. Moreover, natural language processing (NLP) algorithms can analyze donor sentiments from various communication channels, helping nonprofits tailor their messaging to resonate more effectively with their target audience.

Grant writing, a critical aspect of resource acquisition for nonprofits, can also benefit significantly from AI. Natural language generation algorithms can assist in crafting compelling grant proposals by generating clear and persuasive narratives based on data provided by nonprofit professionals.

Finally, communication and promotion of programs are vital for nonprofits to raise awareness and garner support. AI-driven tools can enhance these functions by automating social media posts, tailoring content to specific audience segments, and optimizing the timing of communications for maximum impact. Sentiment analysis algorithms can gauge public reactions to campaigns, helping organizations refine their messaging and outreach strategies. Chatbots with NLP capabilities can engage with stakeholders, providing information about the organization's programs and initiatives. Additionally, AI-powered analytics tools can measure the effectiveness of communication strategies, providing valuable insights for continuous improvement and ensuring that nonprofits can convey their message in a way that resonates with their target audience.

By leveraging AI as a smart partner, nonprofits can harness technology to overcome resource limitations, enhance organizational capabilities, and ultimately increase their positive impact on the communities they serve.

AI and its various applications hold a tremendous transformative power to empower the sector with new resources, processes, and ways that will enhance the efficiency and effectiveness of delivering on their mandate. AI can greatly help address the perennial challenge of resource scarcity.

AI for Good: Empowering Nonprofits With Technology

In the ever-evolving narrative of AI, a new chapter is being written for nonprofit organizations. This chapter reveals how AI is not just a tool for the corporate and scientific realms but a transformative force for the nonprofit sector. A key player in this transformation is data analytics and predictive modeling. Through these AI technologies, nonprofits can decipher vast amounts of data to uncover trends and insights, aiding in more effective donor engagement, resource allocation, and understanding community needs. Predictive models can anticipate future trends, enabling nonprofits to plan proactively.

Another significant aspect of AI in this sector is NLP. This technology, which enables machines to understand and interact with human language, is revolutionizing how nonprofits communicate. From analyzing beneficiary feedback to monitoring social media for public sentiment, NLP provides nonprofits with a deeper connection with their audience and stakeholders.

Machine learning, a subset of AI known for its pattern recognition and decision-making capabilities with minimal human input, is particularly beneficial for program development and evaluation. By learning from past initiatives, machine learning can guide nonprofits in shaping future programs for greater impact. Furthermore, AI is making strides in fundraising and donor management. It empowers nonprofits with the ability to identify potential donors, understand their behaviors, and personalize outreach, thereby enhancing fundraising efforts and donor relationships.

As nonprofits embrace AI, it is crucial to navigate this journey with an ethical compass, ensuring that the use of AI aligns with their core values and mission. This commitment to ethical AI involves ensuring fairness, unbiasedness, and transparency in all AI applications.

In conclusion, AI technologies offer a spectrum of possibilities for nonprofits, from enhancing data analysis to improving stakeholder engagement and program development. As this story unfolds, it's becoming increasingly clear that AI is not an exclusive asset of the for-profit world but a pivotal ally in the narrative of nonprofit innovation and efficiency.

CHAPTER 2

What Is AI?

The rise of powerful AI will be either the best or the worst thing ever to happen to humanity.[1]

—**Stephen Hawking**

The journey through the world of AI is fraught with paradoxes of hope and caution, a sentiment eloquently captured by Stephen Hawking when he said, "The rise of powerful AI will be either the best or the worst thing ever to happen to humanity." This chapter explores that very dichotomy. Hawking's words set the stage for our exploration into the vast and intricate landscape of AI. They remind us of AI's enormous potential to transform our world, offering groundbreaking advancements across diverse sectors. Yet, they also serve as a sobering reminder of the profound responsibilities and ethical considerations accompanying such powerful technologies' development and application. As we embark on this exploration, we navigate the delicate balance between harnessing AI's promise for a better future and understanding the gravity of the challenges it presents.

In this book, we embark on the journey of understanding AI, but with a specific lens. This book is not about delving deep into the engineering intricacies or the complex algorithms that form the backbone of AI and machine learning. Rather, it's akin to opening the hood of a car to get a basic understanding of how the engine works without the intention of becoming a mechanic.

Imagine AI as a sophisticated engine that powers many applications and systems we interact with daily. Just as you don't need to be an automotive engineer to drive a car, you don't need to be an AI expert to understand its impact and applications, especially in the context of nonprofits. We focus on comprehending AI's capabilities, potential uses, and strategic implications for nonprofits. We aim to demystify AI, making it accessible and understandable so that you can appreciate how it can be harnessed to enhance nonprofit organizations' effectiveness, reach, and impact.

In this light, we will explore AI from a strategic perspective, looking at how it can be a powerful tool for problem-solving, decision making, and innovation in the nonprofit sector. We will unravel how AI can automate tasks, provide deep insights from data, and open up new avenues for engagement and service delivery. By the end of this chapter, you should clearly understand what AI is (and isn't), how it's being used today, and how it can be strategically applied in the world of nonprofits.

Really, What Is AI?

Once upon a time, in the vast and intricate world of computer science, a field of study emerged unlike any other—AI. This was not just a new technology or a series of complex algorithms but a grand endeavor to bestow machines with capabilities akin to human intelligence. The creators and visionaries of AI embarked on a journey to make machines smart and intuitive, creating a bridge between human cognition and computational power.

The power of learning and adaptation was at the heart of AI's magic. These machines were not confined to the rigid instructions of traditional programming. Instead, they were designed to learn from experience, much like a child learning to navigate the world. Through a process known as machine learning, these intelligent systems absorbed information, recognized patterns and made decisions. They were like sponges, soaking up data and evolving, continually enhancing their abilities to think, analyze, and solve problems.

AI's capabilities extended into problem-solving, where it shone like a beacon in the night. It could delve into complex scenarios, sifting through mountains of data to unearth solutions that were not evident at first glance. This ability was a game-changer in fields where decisions had to be swift and accurate, with high stakes.

But the true marvel of AI's story lies in its ability to understand and interact with human language. This was the realm of natural language processing (NLP)—a magical bridge that connected the world of machines with the richness of human speech and text. Thanks to NLP, machines began understanding our words, responding to our queries, and even engaging in conversations. This feat blurred the lines between science fiction and reality, bringing to life the fantasy of machines that could talk and listen like humans.

As the tale of AI unfolded, it became clear that this was not just a technological revolution but a new chapter in human innovation and creativity. AI was reshaping how we solved problems, interacted with technology, and envisioned the future. The world watched in awe as AI, once a figment of imaginative minds, turned into a tangible force, opening doors to possibilities that were once the stuff of dreams. And so, the journey of AI continued, each day bringing new advancements and wonders in a story that was only just beginning.

Understanding AI's various types is essential, each representing a different level of complexity and capability. The AI landscape is commonly segmented into three main types: narrow AI, general AI, and artificial superintelligence (ASI). The recent emergence of generative AI adds a new dimension to this categorization.

Narrow AI, also known as Weak AI, is most prevalent in our daily lives. It's designed to perform specific tasks like language translation, voice recognition, or even chess. These systems operate within a limited predefined range and do not possess consciousness or general intelligence. They excel in their designated tasks but cannot transfer their learning or understanding to broader contexts. Examples include chatbots, recommendation engines in e-commerce, and intelligent assistants like Siri or Alexa.

General AI, or strong AI, represents a significant leap from narrow AI. It's a theoretical concept where machines can understand, learn, and apply intelligence broadly and flexibly, just like humans. This form of AI could reason, solve problems, and make judgments across different domains, without being confined to a specific task or function. The development of general AI is still a work in progress, and it remains more of a goal than a reality in AI research.

ASI takes the concept of general AI further. It's a hypothetical scenario where AI surpasses human intelligence in all aspects—from creativity and emotional intelligence to decision making and problem-solving. ASI would be the pinnacle of AI development, offering capabilities beyond our current understanding. However, it also raises profound ethical and existential questions about the future of humanity and AI.

A recent and exciting development in AI is generative AI. This type of AI goes beyond the reactive and functional capabilities of narrow AI, stepping into the realm of creation and innovation. Generative AI can produce content that is entirely new and original, whether it's text, images, or music. Unlike previous forms of AI primarily focused on analysis and decision making based on existing data, generative AI has the potential to innovate and create, pushing the boundaries of AI's role from an assistant to a creator. This form of AI opens up vast possibilities for industries like design, arts, entertainment, and research.

The landscape of AI is diverse and evolving, from the task-specific abilities of narrow AI to the theoretical horizons of general AI and ASI and now to the creative potentials of generative AI. Each type represents a different facet of our quest to imbue machines with intelligence, and each comes with its own set of possibilities and challenges, painting a complex and dynamic picture of AI's role in our world.

Don't fret over the technical complexities of AI. Think of it like driving a car. You don't necessarily need to know the intricacies of the engine, like its size or the number of cylinders, to be an adept driver.

Similarly, a deep understanding of AI's intricate algorithms and inner workings isn't required to utilize or appreciate its potential effectively. Just as you can skillfully navigate a car to your destination, you can harness the benefits of AI in your field, focusing on its applications and impacts rather than the underlying technical details.

What AI Is Not

As we navigate the fascinating world of AI, it's crucial to pause and clarify what AI is not. In our journey through the realms of AI, surrounded by its growing hype and often sensationalized portrayals, we must ground our understanding in reality.

AI Is Not Magic, Nor Is It Science Fiction

Within the imaginative corridors of popular culture, AI is often shrouded in a cloak of mystery and wonder, almost akin to a mystical force or a character straight out of a science fiction novel. In countless movies, books, and media portrayals, AI is depicted as an omnipotent entity, a kind of digital wizard capable of remarkable, almost magical feats. This portrayal can lead to a perception of AI as an all-knowing, all-powerful force, far removed from the limitations of human ability.

However, stepping away from these fantastical narratives, we find that the reality of AI is much more grounded and pragmatic. AI is not a product of sorcery or science fiction; it is born out of human ingenuity and innovation. At its core, AI is a sophisticated blend of algorithms, data, and machine learning techniques. Researchers and engineers meticulously design these algorithms to process information, learn from it, and make decisions or predictions based on that learning.

Contrary to the idea of AI as an entity with magical prowess, it does not possess an inherent, all-encompassing understanding of the world or the universe. AI systems are limited by the scope of their programming and the data they are trained on. They do not have a consciousness or a holistic understanding; they operate within the confines of their designed capabilities.

This misconception of AI as a form of magic or a sci-fi fantasy can lead to unrealistic expectations about its capabilities and roles. Understanding AI for what it truly is—a remarkable technological creation, yet one with defined boundaries and capabilities—is crucial in appreciating its potential and addressing the challenges it presents. AI, as we know it, is a tool created by humans, constantly evolving and improving, but still rooted in the realms of data, algorithms, and the real world.

AI Does Not Possess Consciousness

A pervasive myth is that AI systems possess some form of consciousness or sentience, akin to human beings. This misconception often leads to the belief that these machines can experience thoughts, emotions, and self-awareness, much like humans do. The portrayal of AI in movies and literature as sentient beings with personal desires and feelings only fuels this notion. However, the reality of AI is quite different and far less fantastical.

Even the most sophisticated AI systems in existence today do not have self-awareness or emotional intelligence. These systems, regardless of their complexity or the level of their achievements, operate on the principles of programming, algorithms, and data processing. They are essentially advanced computational tools that analyze patterns, make predictions, or perform tasks based on the data they are fed and the instructions encoded in their algorithms.

Unlike humans, AI lacks the capability for subjective experiences. It does not *feel* joy, sadness, anger, or empathy. The responses of AI systems that might appear emotionally intelligent are the result of carefully designed programming by humans. For example, a chatbot that seems to express sympathy or understanding is merely executing a predefined set of responses aligned with certain keywords or sentiments detected in the user's input.

This distinction is crucial to understanding the capabilities and limitations of AI. While AI can simulate human-like interactions and responses, these are not rooted in genuine consciousness or emotional depth. The machines do not have personal experiences or consciousness; they do not possess an understanding of self. They are devoid of the personal context that shapes human cognition and emotional responses.

Recognizing that AI does not possess consciousness is vital in framing our expectations and interactions with this technology. It helps in appreciating AI's remarkable capabilities while being aware that its *intelligence* is fundamentally different from human intelligence, rooted in data and algorithms rather than conscious thought and emotion.

AI Cannot Replace the Human Touch

Machines have reached remarkable levels of sophistication, enabling them to simulate human-like conversations, recognize speech, and respond to a myriad of queries. This advancement has led to a proliferation of AI applications in customer service, therapy, and even companionship. However, there lies a significant gap between simulation and true replication when it comes to human interaction. In its current form and foreseeable advancements, AI falls short of replicating the genuine depth, empathy, and nuanced understanding that are hallmarks of human interactions.

Human communication is an intricate tapestry woven with threads of emotional subtleties, contextual nuances, nonverbal cues, and cultural contexts. These aspects of communication are deeply rooted in human experiences and emotions. AI, despite its advanced algorithms and data processing capabilities, lacks the ability to comprehend and replicate this level of interaction fully. An AI system might be programmed to recognize sadness in a person's voice and respond with a comforting message, but this response is based on data-driven cues, not genuine empathy or understanding.

The emotional intelligence inherent to humans goes beyond processing information and generating appropriate responses. It involves understanding the complex layers of human emotions, something that AI cannot authentically replicate. Empathy, for instance, is not just about recognizing an emotion and responding to it; it's about sharing and understanding the experience of another person on a deeper, more personal level.

Moreover, the subtleties in human relationships, such as trust, understanding, and genuine care, are built over time through shared experiences and emotional connections. These aspects of human relationships are beyond the realm of AI's capabilities. While AI can provide assistance and even mimic certain aspects of human interaction, it cannot replace the genuine connections and understanding that develop in human relationships.

While AI has made impressive strides in simulating human-like interactions, it is important to recognize its limitations in this area. The depth, empathy, and nuanced understanding of human interactions are unique to our species and are what fundamentally differentiate us from machines. Recognizing this distinction helps us appreciate the value of human touch in our interactions and relationships, something that AI cannot authentically replicate or replace.

AI Is Not Infallible

AI often emerges as a beacon of precision and sophistication. There exists a prevailing notion that AI systems, with their complex algorithms and data-processing capabilities, are infallible and impeccably accurate. This perception, however, overlooks a critical aspect of AI—its inherent susceptibility to flaws and biases, which stem from its very nature and creation process.

AI systems, at their core, are crafted by humans and are only as good as the data they are trained on. They are not inherently equipped with an understanding of the world; rather, they learn from patterns and information fed to them. This learning process makes them vulnerable to the biases present in their training data. If the data are skewed, incomplete, or biased, the AI system will inadvertently reflect these imperfections in its outputs and decisions. For instance, an AI model trained on historical hiring data that contain biases against certain groups may perpetuate these biases in its candidate selection process.

Moreover, the design and programming of AI systems are subject to the limitations and perspectives of their creators. Human programmers, with their own sets of experiences and biases, craft the algorithms and make decisions about which data to include or exclude. These decisions, whether conscious or unconscious, shape the behavior and outcomes of the AI systems. As a result, the potential for human error and oversight is inherently woven into the fabric of AI technology.

Another aspect to consider is the dynamic and ever-changing nature of the world. AI systems, especially those operating in complex and variable environments, may not always adapt quickly or accurately to new or unforeseen situations. They may excel in controlled environments or specific tasks but falter when faced with novel or ambiguous scenarios.

While AI represents a monumental leap in technology, offering immense benefits in efficiency and analytics, it is not a panacea. Recognizing AI's susceptibility to errors, biases, and limitations is crucial. This understanding underscores the importance of continual monitoring, evaluation, and updating of AI systems, along with a thoughtful consideration of their deployment. It also highlights the essential role of human oversight in ensuring that AI is used responsibly and ethically, complementing rather than replacing human judgment and expertise.

AI Does Not Independently Make Decisions

There's a common misconception that AI systems possess their own will or consciousness, enabling them to make independent decisions. This notion often arises from portrayals of AI in science fiction, where machines are depicted as having autonomous thoughts and desires.

However, the reality of AI's decision-making process is grounded in a much more controlled and predetermined framework.

AI systems, regardless of their complexity or the sophistication of their outputs, operate based on a set of predefined algorithms and data analysis. These algorithms are essentially a series of instructions created by humans, guiding how the AI processes information and responds to various inputs. The *decisions* made by AI systems are essentially the outcomes of these algorithmic processes, heavily reliant on the data they have been trained on and the parameters set by their developers.

For instance, when an AI system *decides* to recommend a particular product to a consumer, it is not making a conscious choice. Rather, it analyzes data patterns from the consumer's past behaviors, preferences indicated by similar users, and other relevant data points. The recommendation is the product of a calculated analysis, aligned with the goals and functions encoded into the AI by its creators.

This distinction is vital to understand, particularly when considering the integration of AI into critical sectors like health care, finance, or law enforcement. In these fields, the decisions made by AI can have significant impacts. As such, human oversight becomes crucial. It ensures that the decisions are not only based on logical data processing but also consider ethical, moral, and societal implications that are beyond the scope of AI's programmed understanding.

Furthermore, the responsibility for the actions and decisions of AI systems ultimately lies in human hands. While AI can process information and provide outputs, it does not bear accountability. The designers, operators, and users of AI systems are responsible for how these systems are used and the consequences of their use.

While AI can analyze data and provide solutions or recommendations, it does not independently make decisions in the way humans do. Understanding this limitation is crucial in managing expectations around AI's role and ensuring responsible usage. It underscores the importance of maintaining human involvement and oversight in AI-driven systems, particularly in areas with significant societal impact.

AI Is Not a Universal Panacea

The term *panacea* originates from Greek mythology, referring to a remedy that could cure all diseases and prolong life indefinitely. In modern times, the concept is used metaphorically to describe a solution that seems to answer a vast array of problems. When it comes to AI, there is often a misconception that it acts as this sort of panacea—a universal solution to a broad spectrum of challenges across various sectors. However, the reality of AI's capabilities and applications is far more nuanced.

AI, in its current form, is not a magic bullet that can solve all problems or be effectively applied to every situation. Its effectiveness and utility are heavily contingent upon the context in which it is deployed, the quality of data it is fed, and the specific nature of the problems it is tasked to address. AI systems learn and make decisions based on the data they process. If these data are limited, biased, or of poor quality, the AI's effectiveness is significantly compromised.

For instance, in the health care sector, AI shows great promise in areas like diagnostic imaging and patient data analysis. However, its efficacy is highly dependent on the availability of comprehensive, accurate, and diverse data sets. Without this, AI's ability to assist health care professionals and improve patient outcomes is limited.

Similarly, in the realm of autonomous vehicles, AI can potentially revolutionize transportation. However, this application requires not only sophisticated AI algorithms but also a host of other factors like regulatory approval, infrastructure changes, and public acceptance. AI alone is not enough to overcome these multifaceted challenges.

Moreover, the nature of the problem itself plays a critical role in determining the suitability of AI as a solution. AI is excellent at processing large volumes of data and identifying patterns, making it ideal for applications like fraud detection or market analysis. However, it is less effective in situations that require deep understanding, empathy, or creative thinking—qualities that are currently exclusive to human cognition.

While AI is a powerful tool with the potential to transform numerous aspects of our society, it is important to maintain realistic expectations about its capabilities. Recognizing that AI is not a universal panacea helps in understanding its limitations and potential. It encourages a more thoughtful and strategic approach to its implementation, ensuring that AI is used where it can be most effective and beneficial.

AI operates within certain boundaries. It's a tool, a product of human creation, and not an autonomous entity. Understanding what AI is not is just as important as understanding what it is. It helps set realistic expectations and appreciate AI's true nature and potential in our world.

CHAPTER 3

Harnessing Innovation

Fresh Approaches in Nonprofit Management

There's a way to do it better—find it.[1]

—Thomas A. Edison

In the vast and varied world of the nonprofit sector, home to over 10 million organizations globally, the quest to serve billions of people with diverse needs brings to mind Thomas A. Edison's inspiring words: "There's a way to do it better—find it." This phrase holds special significance for nonprofits, which find themselves in a landscape that's always shifting.

The environments they operate in, the needs of the communities they support, and the resources at their disposal are continually changing. It's a world that never stands still, demanding constant innovation and flexibility.

Think of each nonprofit as a navigator in an ocean of change, where adapting to the tides is not just advisable but essential. Edison's encouragement to find better ways is more than a motivational quote in this context; it's a fundamental principle. It urges these organizations to look at problems from fresh angles, question the status quo, and boldly venture into new solutions. It's about being open to change, whether it's adopting a new technology, rethinking a fundraising strategy, or finding more efficient ways to deliver services.

The need for continuous improvement in the nonprofit sector isn't just about fine-tuning operations; it's at the heart of their mission. The goal is to amplify their impact, touch more lives, and make a deeper, more meaningful difference. In a world brimming with complex challenges, the ability to find and forge better paths is invaluable. Whether it's addressing poverty, education, health, or environmental issues, the pursuit of doing things better is what drives the sector forward. It's about harnessing creativity, embracing new ideas, and continually striving to enhance the way they serve and support their communities. This journey of constant improvement and adaptation is what enables nonprofits to not just make a difference, but to expand their reach and deepen their impact in a world that needs it most.

What Is Innovation?

Innovation in the nonprofit sector unfolds as a compelling narrative of creativity and resilience. It's the art and science of bringing new ideas to life, crafting dynamic solutions, and discovering more effective methods to address the broad tapestry of social challenges. When we speak of innovation in this context, it's not confined to the realms of cutting-edge technology or groundbreaking scientific discoveries. Instead, it's about reimagining traditional approaches, whether it's in service delivery, fundraising, or community engagement, and reshaping them in ways that enhance impact and efficiency.

Think of innovation in nonprofits as a journey rather than a destination. It involves taking a step back from the well-trodden path to explore uncharted territories. This could mean adapting a strategy from the business sector to boost fundraising efforts, using data analytics to tailor programs more effectively to beneficiary needs, or employing social media in novel ways to galvanize community support. It's about being agile and responsive, willing to experiment, and learn from both successes and setbacks.

Innovation in this sector is driven by a deep understanding of the unique challenges and opportunities that nonprofits face. It's about stretching limited resources, maximizing reach, and making every effort count. It's finding that sweet spot where creativity meets purpose, leading to solutions that are not only effective but also sustainable and scalable.

At its core, innovation within nonprofits is fueled by the passion to make a difference and the determination to find better ways of doing so. It's an ongoing process of refinement and evolution, with the ultimate goal of enriching lives and fostering positive change in communities around the world. In the end, innovation in the nonprofit sector is less about the flash of newness and more about the enduring glow of progress and impact.

Trailblazing Examples From the Nonprofit Sector

Innovation isn't just a buzzword; it's a key to making a real difference. Across the globe, these organizations are coming up with creative ways to tackle big problems. From using new tech like AI to protect endangered animals, to finding better ways to bring in donations through the Internet, nonprofits are showing us how thinking outside the box can lead to big changes. This world of nonprofit innovation is all about finding new solutions to old problems, reaching more people, and making a bigger impact in the communities they serve. Let's explore some exemplary practices.

Mobile Health Clinics

Mobile health clinics represent a significant innovation in bringing health care to remote and underserved areas, a challenge that many nonprofits, including doctors without borders, are tackling head-on. These mobile clinics are more than just vehicles equipped with medical supplies; they are technologically advanced centers that enable telemedicine services. By connecting with specialists across the globe through technology, health care professionals operating these clinics can offer a level of medical expertise that was once impossible in remote regions.

This approach not only broadens the reach of quality health care but also ensures that residents in these areas have access to specialized medical consultations and treatments. These mobile clinics are a testament to how innovative solutions and technology can be harnessed to bridge gaps in health care accessibility, bringing vital medical services to those who need them the most, regardless of their geographical location.

Digital Fundraising Platforms

The advent of digital fundraising platforms has brought about a transformative shift in the nonprofit sector, fundamentally changing how organizations connect with donors and raise funds. Platforms such as GoFundMe, Kickstarter, and JustGiving have opened new avenues for nonprofits to reach out to a global audience. These platforms provide a space where organizations can vividly share their stories, missions, and the impacts of their work, thereby forging a deeper emotional connection with potential donors. This storytelling aspect, coupled with the ease and convenience of online donations, has significantly simplified the giving process, encouraging more people to contribute.

Furthermore, the virality potential of digital campaigns means that nonprofits can now tap into networks far beyond their traditional spheres, exponentially increasing their fundraising potential and, in turn, their capacity to make a difference in their cause areas. This shift to digital platforms represents not just an adaptation to the digital age but a strategic move to harness the power of technology and community to fuel their philanthropic missions.

Blockchain for Transparency

In recent years, the integration of blockchain technology in the nonprofit sector has marked a significant stride toward enhancing transparency and accountability in charitable donations. Leading this innovative approach are organizations like BitGive, which have recognized the potential of blockchain to revolutionize how donations are tracked and managed. Blockchain technology, at its core, is a decentralized ledger that records transactions in a secure and transparent manner. By applying this technology to charitable donations, organizations enable donors to track their contributions in real time. This means that when a donor makes a contribution to a cause, they can see exactly how their funds are being utilized, following the journey of their donation from the moment it leaves their hands to when it reaches the intended recipients or is used in a specific project.

This level of transparency is groundbreaking. It addresses one of the long-standing concerns in the philanthropic world: the uncertainty about how donations are used. By providing a clear trail, blockchain technology reassures donors that their contributions are indeed making an impact in the intended way. This not only strengthens trust in the organization but also encourages a culture of accountability and integrity in the management of funds.

This innovative use of blockchain in the nonprofit sector can potentially attract a new demographic of donors who value transparency and digital engagement. It aligns with a growing trend of donor expectations for greater openness and measurable impact from charitable organizations. In essence, the adoption of blockchain technology by nonprofits like BitGive signifies a progressive shift toward more transparent, efficient, and trust-based philanthropic practices, paving the way for a new era of engaged and informed giving.

Social Media for Advocacy

The utilization of social media for advocacy has emerged as a powerful tool in the arsenal of nonprofit organizations. In today's digital age, social media platforms offer an unprecedented opportunity for these organizations to amplify their voices, rally support, and drive tangible societal change. A prime example of this is the #MeToo movement, which brilliantly leveraged social media to shine a light on the pervasive issue of sexual harassment and assault.

Through platforms like Twitter, Facebook, and Instagram, the #MeToo movement transcended geographical boundaries, encouraging individuals from all over the world to share their stories and experiences. This movement underscored the power of social media in unifying voices, creating a collective force that could no longer be ignored. The sheer volume of personal stories and the visibility they garnered through these platforms led to a global conversation, bringing about a heightened awareness and a shift in societal attitudes toward sexual misconduct.

This approach to advocacy demonstrates how social media can be an effective tool for nonprofits not just in raising awareness but in fostering community, solidarity, and action. By creating a space where voices can be heard and stories can be shared, nonprofits can engage with a broader audience, mobilize grassroots movements, and influence public opinion and policy. In a world where information and communication technologies are ever-evolving, the strategic use of social media for advocacy empowers nonprofits to reach wider, engage deeper, and impact greater, driving social change in ways that were once unimaginable.

AI in Wildlife Conservation

The integration of AI in wildlife conservation represents a groundbreaking shift in how conservation efforts are conducted. Organizations like the Wildlife Conservation Society are at the forefront of this innovative approach, employing AI to enhance their monitoring and protection of endangered species. By utilizing AI technology to analyze images from camera traps, they are able to process vast amounts of visual data more efficiently and accurately than ever before.

In the vast and often inaccessible stretches of wilderness where these camera traps are placed, they capture thousands of images of wildlife. Manually sorting through this sheer volume of data to identify species, track their movements, and monitor their behavior is an enormously time-consuming task. AI dramatically streamlines this process. It employs sophisticated algorithms capable of recognizing different species, counting individuals, and even identifying unique animals. This not only speeds up the data analysis but also improves the accuracy of the findings, providing conservationists with vital information about population sizes, habitat use, and potential threats to wildlife.

Moreover, AI's ability to rapidly analyze images and provide real-time data is crucial in anti-poaching efforts. It enables conservationists to respond more swiftly to potential threats, offering a greater chance of protecting at-risk species. This innovative use of AI in wildlife conservation is not just enhancing the efficiency of existing practices; it's opening up new possibilities for understanding and safeguarding the natural world.

The adoption of AI in wildlife conservation exemplifies how technology can be harnessed for environmental stewardship, offering a beacon of hope for the preservation of our planet's biodiversity. It's a clear testament to how AI can be a powerful ally in the fight to protect and preserve the world's endangered species.

Interactive Educational Tools

The revolution in the educational landscape brought about by interactive educational tools has been nothing short of transformative, particularly in the way knowledge is accessed and disseminated globally. Spearheading this revolution are organizations like Khan Academy, which have harnessed the power of digital technology to democratize education. By offering free online courses and a suite of interactive tools, they have broken down traditional barriers to education, making high-quality learning resources accessible to all, regardless of location or economic status.

Khan Academy's platform exemplifies the innovative use of digital technology in education. Its interactive tools are designed not just to impart knowledge, but to engage learners actively, adapting to individual learning styles and paces. This personalized approach makes learning more effective and enjoyable, encouraging learners to explore and absorb information at their own rhythm.

Perhaps most importantly, these digital education platforms have been a boon for underprivileged areas where access to quality education is often limited. By making educational content available online for free, Khan Academy and similar platforms have opened up opportunities for learners who might otherwise have limited access to schooling or educational resources. This accessibility is critical in bridging educational gaps and promoting lifelong learning, empowering individuals with the knowledge and skills needed to improve their life circumstances.

The impact of these interactive educational tools extends beyond individual learning; it has the potential to uplift entire communities by providing the next generation with the education necessary for personal and professional development. In this way, organizations leveraging digital education tools are not just educating individuals; they are contributing to the broader goal of global educational equity.

Renewable Energy Projects

Nonprofits like The Solar Foundation are working on renewable energy projects, helping communities, especially in developing countries, access clean and sustainable energy sources. The push toward renewable energy projects by nonprofits like The Solar Foundation marks a significant stride in addressing both environmental and social issues globally. These organizations are at the forefront of a movement that seeks to bring sustainable and clean energy sources to communities, with a particular focus on developing countries where access to reliable and affordable energy is often a challenge. By championing renewable energy projects, these nonprofits are not just advocating for environmental sustainability;

they are also working to transform the quality of life for countless individuals.

In many developing regions, the lack of reliable energy sources can impede economic development, education, and health care. The introduction of renewable energy solutions, such as solar power, offers a viable and sustainable alternative. These projects can provide consistent electricity, which is a catalyst for improving education outcomes, as schools can operate more effectively; health care facilities can offer better services with reliable power for essential equipment; and small businesses can flourish with extended operating hours.

The focus on renewable energy aligns with global efforts to combat climate change. By reducing reliance on fossil fuels and promoting the use of clean energy, these projects contribute significantly to the reduction of carbon emissions. This not only has a positive impact on the global environment but also on local ecosystems and the health of community members.

The work of nonprofits in renewable energy projects often goes beyond just the installation of solar panels or wind turbines. They engage in community education and capacity building, ensuring that locals understand the technology and can maintain and manage these renewable energy sources independently. This approach ensures the sustainability of projects and empowers communities with the knowledge and tools to take control of their energy futures.

The involvement of nonprofits in renewable energy projects represents a holistic approach to development and environmental stewardship. It's an effort that addresses immediate needs like energy access while contributing to long-term goals of sustainability and climate change mitigation. Through these initiatives, nonprofits are lighting the way toward a brighter, cleaner future for communities around the world.

Can Small Nonprofits Be Innovative?

Absolutely, small nonprofits not only can be innovative but indeed must embrace innovation as a key strategy for their sustainability and growth. In the highly competitive realm of the nonprofit sector, organizations of all sizes find themselves vying for attention, funding, and impact. For small nonprofits, this competition is often more intense due to their limited resources. This constraint, however, can become a catalyst for creativity and innovation.

Unlike their larger counterparts, small nonprofits typically have more flexibility and less bureaucracy, allowing them to adapt quickly, experiment with new ideas, and implement changes without the complex layers of approval that can slow down larger organizations. This agility is a significant advantage in a sector where the ability to respond promptly to emerging needs and changes in the environment can make a huge difference.

Moreover, small nonprofits often cultivate closer connections with their communities. This proximity can lead to a deeper understanding of the specific needs and nuances of their target populations, enabling them to tailor innovative solutions that are more effective and impactful. Personalized approaches, grassroots initiatives, and community-driven solutions are areas where small nonprofits can excel, turning their size into a strength.

Innovation for small nonprofits also often means finding creative ways to maximize their resources. This can include forming strategic partnerships, leveraging volunteer skills, or utilizing technology to amplify their reach and efficiency. Social media, for instance, offers a low-cost, high-impact channel for fundraising, advocacy, and community engagement.

The necessity for innovation in small nonprofits goes beyond just keeping up with the sector; it's about carving out a niche, making a unique impact, and ensuring long-term sustainability. In essence, embracing innovation is not just a choice but an imperative for small nonprofits aiming to thrive in a dynamic and challenging environment.

Innovation Culture

Building a culture of innovation within nonprofit organizations is a critical endeavor, yet it often faces the challenge of time scarcity. Many nonprofits operate under the notion that they cannot afford to invest in innovation due to their limited resources. The pressure to utilize every minute and every dollar toward immediate service delivery is immense. However, this perspective, while understandable, overlooks the long-term benefits and necessity of fostering an innovative environment.

Encouraging nonprofits to embrace innovation involves shifting the mindset from seeing innovation as a luxury to viewing it as an essential component of sustainability and growth. Yes, resources in the nonprofit sector are often stretched thin, but investing in innovation doesn't always mean significant financial expenditure. It can be as simple as dedicating time for staff to brainstorm new ideas, encouraging experimentation with new approaches, or even reallocating existing resources to try out innovative solutions.

A culture of innovation also means embracing a degree of risk-taking and accepting that not every new idea will lead to success. It's about learning from failures as much as from successes and viewing each as an opportunity for growth. This mindset shift is crucial for nonprofits to evolve and remain relevant in a rapidly changing world.

Furthermore, innovation can lead to greater efficiency and impact in the long run. By finding new ways to solve problems, nonprofits can enhance their services, reach more beneficiaries, and make their resources go further. This doesn't mean diverting attention from immediate goals but rather integrating innovative thinking into the daily operations and strategic planning of the organization.

Building a culture of innovation in nonprofits is about balancing the immediate needs of service delivery with the long-term vision of the organization. It's about recognizing that investing time and resources in innovation is not just beneficial but necessary for navigating the challenges and opportunities of the nonprofit sector.

It's a common scenario in the nonprofit sector: organizations are deeply immersed in their day-to-day operations, often due to the pressing nature of the needs they address and the limited resources at their disposal. This intense focus on immediate operational tasks can lead to a situation where there's little time or interest left to step back and consider alternative, potentially more effective ways of achieving their goals. The drive to meet immediate demands often takes precedence, leaving scant room for exploring innovative approaches or strategic planning.

This operational tunnel vision, while understandable given the constraints many nonprofits operate under, can sometimes mean missed opportunities for improvement and growth. Stepping back to evaluate processes, strategies, and outcomes isn't just about taking a break from the action; it's a crucial exercise in ensuring that the organization's efforts are as impactful as possible. It involves asking critical questions: Are there more efficient ways to operate? Can new technologies or method-ologies enhance our impact? Are we effectively meeting the needs of those we serve, and how can we do better?

Allocating time and resources to this kind of reflective practice can be challenging, especially when resources are stretched thin. However, the long-term benefits—such as improved efficiency, stronger impact, and greater sustainability—can far outweigh the immediate costs. Encouraging a culture where periodic stepping back and reassessment is valued can lead to significant advancements in how these organizations fulfill their missions. It's about balancing the urgent with the important, ensuring that the day-to-day operations are not just well-executed but are also aligned with the most effective and impactful strategies.

A notable example of a nonprofit organization that successfully stepped back to reassess and innovate their operations is Charity: Water. This organization, dedicated to providing clean and safe drinking water to people in developing countries, faced the challenge of proving to donors that their contributions were having a tangible impact.

Traditionally, like many nonprofits, Charity: Water was primarily focused on the immediate goal of fundraising and implementing water projects. However, they recognized the importance of transparency and donor engagement as key factors for long-term sustainability and impact. To address this, they decided to innovate by leveraging technology.

Charity: Water started using GPS technology to provide donors with the exact locations of the wells they funded. They also implemented remote sensors in their water projects to monitor and ensure their continued functioning. This not only provided transparency but also allowed them to collect data to improve their operations. By taking the time to innovate in how they reported back to donors and monitored projects, Charity: Water enhanced donor trust and engagement, leading to increased funding and, consequently, the ability to help more communities.

This example illustrates how stepping back from day-to-day operations to explore and implement new ways of doing things can significantly benefit a nonprofit organization. Charity: Water's approach to incorporating technology for transparency and accountability shows that even small innovations, when thoughtfully executed, can lead to substantial improvements in effectiveness and growth.

Where to Start

Innovation, particularly in the nonprofit sector, isn't a spontaneous occurrence but rather a result of intentional effort and allocation of resources. It requires a conscious commitment from the organization, underlining the fact that innovative ideas and approaches don't simply materialize out of thin air.

To foster an environment where innovation can thrive, nonprofits need to dedicate time to brainstorming, experimenting, and exploring new possibilities. This investment goes beyond just financial resources; it includes dedicating staff time for research and development, creating spaces for creative thinking, and encouraging a culture where innovative ideas are valued and tested.

Successful innovation, particularly in the nonprofit sector, is intrinsically linked to the willingness to venture beyond the familiar territories of conventional practices. It's about embracing the new and unknown, and being open to change, which often means challenging the status quo and traditional ways of thinking. This journey outside the comfort zone is not without its risks, but successful innovation hinges on the ability to take these risks in a calculated manner. It's about weighing the potential benefits against the risks and having the courage to move forward, even when the path isn't fully clear.

Innovation also involves a continuous learning process. It's recognizing that not every new idea or approach will lead to success, and being prepared to learn from both the triumphs and setbacks. These experiences, be they successes or failures, are invaluable in refining strategies and approaches, contributing to a deeper understanding of what works and what doesn't. It's a cycle of trying, learning, and evolving that drives meaningful change and improvement.

Coupling this innovative mindset with the right resources is key. Resources here don't just refer to funding but also to time, talent, and tools. It's about allocating the necessary time for team members to brainstorm and experiment, ensuring there are skilled individuals who can drive the innovation process, and providing the tools and technologies needed to bring new ideas to life. This strategic focus on resources is what turns innovative ideas from mere concepts into actionable and impactful initiatives.

For organizations in the nonprofit sector looking to harness the power of innovation, the initial step is to recognize and accept that innovation is a deliberate and strategic process. It requires a commitment not just in terms of resources but also in mindset and approach. By acknowledging this and dedicating the necessary focus and resources, nonprofits can pave the way for transformative ideas that significantly enhance their impact and effectiveness in their missions.

As a practical tactic, benchmarking and learning from best practices on a global scale represent critical steps for nonprofits aiming to elevate their impact and effectiveness. This approach goes beyond mere observation; it involves actively seeking out and analyzing successful strategies and models from around the world. In doing so, nonprofits can compare their methods and outcomes with those of similar organizations globally, drawing valuable lessons and insights.

AI plays a pivotal role in enhancing this benchmarking process. With AI, nonprofits can sift through extensive datasets that span geographical boundaries, extracting relevant information about best practices, innovative strategies, and effective solutions employed in different parts of the world. For instance, an organization working in public health can use AI to analyze and learn from global health initiatives, understand the factors contributing to their success, and identify ways to apply these learnings to their own initiatives.

Moreover, AI facilitates a deeper analysis by not just collating data but also identifying patterns, trends, and correlations within this data. This capability is particularly beneficial in understanding the nuances of why certain strategies work in some contexts and not in others. Such insights are invaluable in tailoring global best practices to fit local needs and circumstances.

Beyond analysis, AI also aids in the continuous monitoring of an organization's performance against international benchmarks. This is crucial for maintaining high standards and ensuring that the organization is not operating in a vacuum. Regularly comparing one's strategies and outcomes with global benchmarks keeps an organization aligned with the best, most effective practices and can inspire continuous improvement.

Incorporating AI into global benchmarking practices empowers nonprofits to break down geographical and informational barriers. It enables them to harness a wealth of global knowledge and experience, adapt and refine their strategies, and stay at the forefront of innovation in their field. For nonprofits committed to making a significant impact, embracing AI in benchmarking and learning from global best practices is not just an option; it's a pathway to achieving greater success and sustainability in their missions.

Can AI Support Innovation?

AI can be a powerful ally in supporting innovation, especially for organizations looking to break new ground. Think of AI as a smart assistant that's great at handling data and spotting patterns. For example, when you have a lot of information—like feedback from the community you serve or statistics on how well your programs are doing—AI can quickly sort through it all and highlight what's important. This can give you new insights, like finding out which parts of your program are working best or identifying new needs in your community that you haven't noticed before.

AI can also take over routine tasks, like organizing files or scheduling, which frees up your team's time to focus on more creative work. It's like having an extra pair of hands to do the heavy lifting, so you can spend more time brainstorming and coming up with innovative ideas.

Plus, AI can help you try out these new ideas faster. It can simulate different scenarios or predict how changes might play out, giving you a clearer picture of what might happen without risking actual resources. In a way, AI is like a sandbox where you can play around with different strategies and see what works best.

If we liken innovation to a boat that ventures into the vast seas of possibility, then AI can be seen as the sail that propels it forward. Just as a sail harnesses the wind's power to navigate and speed up a boat's journey, AI captures and utilizes the vast currents of data and technology to drive innovation more swiftly and effectively. In the nonprofit sector, where resources are often limited and challenges vast, AI can provide the necessary momentum to explore new horizons. It aids in navigating through complex data waters, bringing insights to the surface that can spark creative solutions and strategic decision making. In this analogy, while the boat—innovation—is the essential vessel for change and progress, the sail—AI—is a crucial tool that amplifies the effort, making the journey not only faster but also more impactful.

So, in short, yes, AI can be a big support in driving innovation. It offers new ways of looking at data, saves time on routine tasks, and helps test out new ideas safely. All of these can be a huge boost when you're trying to come up with fresh, effective ways to make a difference.

CHAPTER 4

Seven Fundamental Nonprofit Management Functions

Not everything that counts can be counted, and not everything that can be counted counts.[1]

—William Bruce Cameron

In this chapter, we delve into the seven fundamental nonprofit management functions, essential elements that form the backbone of effective and impactful nonprofit organizations. Guided by William Bruce Cameron's insightful words, "Not everything that counts can be counted, and not everything that can be counted counts," we explore the multifaceted nature of nonprofit management. This quote reminds us that while some aspects of management are easily quantifiable, the true essence of a nonprofit's impact often lies in the intangible, the unquantifiable. It's a realm where passion meets purpose, and success transcends mere numbers. From governance to resource development, each function we discuss plays a crucial role in translating an organization's mission into meaningful action. These functions, while distinct, work synergistically to ensure that nonprofits not only survive but thrive and make a lasting difference in the communities they serve.

There is a general misperception that managing a nonprofit is simpler than running a for-profit business. This assumption often stems from the belief that nonprofits, primarily driven by mission rather than profit, face fewer complexities. However, this is a significant underestimation of the challenges inherent in nonprofit management. Nonprofit leaders must navigate a unique set of challenges: they grapple with limited resources while striving to maximize impact, balance the expectations of diverse stakeholders, and adhere to stringent regulatory and funding requirements. Moreover, they often operate in environments of high uncertainty and change, requiring a nimble and adaptive management approach. The need for strategic planning, financial acumen, and operational efficiency in nonprofits is as critical as in any for-profit organization. Additionally, nonprofit managers must foster a culture that aligns with their mission and values, which often involves inspiring and mobilizing a workforce that includes a substantial number of volunteers. This complexity in nonprofit management is frequently underestimated, leading to a gap in understanding the skills, dedication, and strategic thinking required to lead such organizations effectively.

One prominent example of a large nonprofit organization that exemplifies the complexity of nonprofit management is the American

Red Cross. Known globally for its disaster relief efforts, blood donation drives, and humanitarian aid, the American Red Cross operates on a scale comparable to a large for-profit corporation, requiring sophisticated management strategies.

The complexity of managing an organization like the American Red Cross lies in its broad scope of services, extensive network of volunteers, and the logistical challenges of responding to emergencies and disasters across the world. Coordinating efforts across various domains—from immediate disaster response to long-term recovery, health services, and community preparedness programs—demands a high level of strategic planning and operational efficiency.

Financial management is another area of complexity. The organization must efficiently allocate its resources, often sourced from a mix of individual donations, government grants, and corporate partnerships, to various programs while ensuring transparency and accountability to its donors and stakeholders.

Furthermore, managing a vast workforce composed largely of volunteers adds another layer of complexity. The American Red Cross must constantly engage and train thousands of volunteers, aligning their efforts with the organization's mission and operational needs.

These challenges illustrate that the American Red Cross, like many large nonprofits, operates with a level of complexity that requires sophisticated management skills, strategic foresight, and a deep understanding of both humanitarian work and organizational dynamics. This complexity often goes unrecognized by those outside the nonprofit sector, who may not see the intricate balancing act these organizations perform in delivering their services and achieving their mission.

In the same vein, the notion that smaller nonprofits, such as a local food bank, are simpler to manage is another common misconception. While they may operate on a smaller scale compared to larger organizations, the complexities they face are proportionally significant and often mirror those of bigger nonprofits in many respects.

A local food bank, for instance, deals with a myriad of challenges that require a nuanced approach to management. First, there's the critical task of resource development and management. They must secure a consistent supply of food, which involves building and maintaining relationships with donors, local businesses, and community members. This requires strategic planning and effective communication, similar to larger organizations.

Financial management is another area of complexity for such small organizations. Local food banks usually operate with a limited budget and must make every dollar count. They need to ensure financial sustainability while being transparent and accountable to their donors and the community they serve.

Additionally, they face operational challenges such as inventory management, volunteer coordination, and ensuring the equitable distribution of food to those in need. Managing these operations efficiently is crucial to their effectiveness and impact.

Moreover, small nonprofits must navigate the same regulatory and compliance issues as larger ones. They are subject to laws and regulations governing nonprofits, which require compliance and often detailed reporting. In essence, the management of a small nonprofit like a local food bank, while different in scale, is similar in complexity to larger organizations. They must effectively juggle resource constraints, operational challenges, and strategic planning, all while staying true to their mission and serving their communities. This complexity is often underestimated, underscoring the need for skilled management and strategic thinking in nonprofits of all sizes.

The model illustrated in Figure 4.1 serves as an insightful framework for understanding the multifaceted nature of nonprofit management, encapsulating seven core functions that are essential for effective operation and success. These functions include governance, strategic planning and implementation, resource development, financial management, program development and project management, stakeholder management, marketing and communication, and human resource management (HRM). Each leaf of the model represents a distinct area, yet they are all interconnected, contributing to the overall health and effectiveness of the nonprofit organization.

In our exploration of these functions, we will delve into how AI can significantly contribute to each one of them. From enhancing

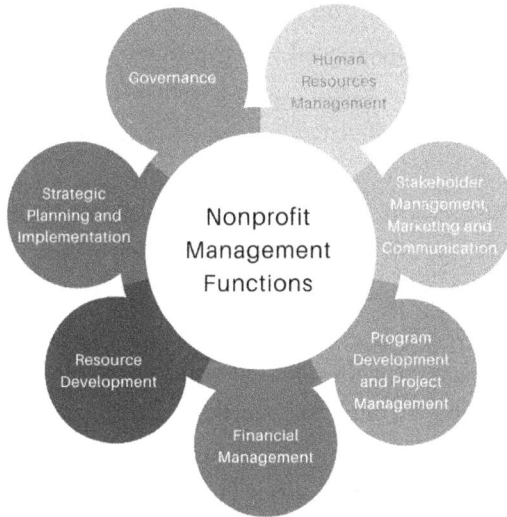

Figure 4.1 Nonprofit management functions

decision making in governance to streamlining operations in program management, and from augmenting resource development strategies to optimizing stakeholder engagement, AI has the potential to revolutionize traditional approaches in nonprofit management. By leveraging AI's capabilities, nonprofits can achieve greater efficiency, impact, and sustainability, aligning with their mission and adapting to the evolving demands of the sector. This intersection of nonprofit management functions with AI technology represents a frontier of opportunities, promising transformative changes in how nonprofits operate and thrive.

Governance

Effective governance is indeed the cornerstone of a nonprofit organization's success and sustainability. It hinges on the strategic direction and oversight provided by the board of directors or trustees, who bear the responsibility of aligning the organization's activities with its mission, vision, and values. They also play a crucial role in overseeing executive management and ensuring compliance with legal, ethical, and financial standards. For governance to be effective, it requires a board that is not only diverse and skilled but also equipped with clear and transparent communication channels. This diverse composition enables a variety of perspectives, enhancing the decision-making process and ensuring that the organization is well-equipped to navigate the myriad challenges and changes in the nonprofit sector. Strong governance fosters organizational growth, builds donor confidence, and enhances the delivery of impactful services.

AI can significantly contribute to strengthening governance in several ways. AI can aid in data-driven decision making by providing detailed analytics and insights on various aspects of the organization's operations. For instance, AI tools can analyze donor data, financial reports, and market trends, offering valuable information that can guide strategic planning and policy making. These insights help ensure that decisions are based on comprehensive and up-to-date information, leading to more effective and strategic outcomes.

AI can streamline and optimize various governance processes. For example, AI-driven tools can assist in monitoring compliance with regulations and standards, reducing the risk of legal or ethical breaches. AI can also be used to enhance board communications, facilitating more efficient meeting preparations, minute-taking, and follow-up actions, thereby improving overall governance efficiency.

Furthermore, AI can assist in predicting future trends and potential challenges, enabling the board to proactively plan and adapt to changing circumstances. This predictive capability is particularly valuable in strategic planning, risk management, and resource allocation, ensuring that the organization is well-prepared for future developments.

By integrating AI into governance practices, nonprofit organizations can achieve a higher level of efficiency and effectiveness in their decision making and strategic planning. AI's capabilities in data analysis, predictive modeling, and process optimization make it an invaluable tool for enhancing the quality of governance and ensuring the long-term success and sustainability of the organization.

Strategic Planning and Implementation

Strategic planning in the nonprofit sector is a critical process that sets the course for an organization's future. It involves establishing long-term goals and charting a path to achieve them. This process necessitates a thorough understanding of the organization's current position and capacity, as well as a clear vision of where it aims to be in the future. Strategic evaluation, a key component of this process, assesses the organization's present state and identifies the steps needed to reach its desired future state. The resulting strategic plan acts as a roadmap, guiding the development of operational plans and ensuring alignment with the organization's overarching goals.

Moreover, strategic planning is deeply rooted in stakeholder engagement. It's vital to incorporate the perspectives of donors, beneficiaries, staff, and the community to create a plan that is both reflective of their needs and aspirations and realistic in its expectations. Engaging these stakeholders not only ensures a more comprehensive planning process but also fosters a sense of ownership and commitment to the plan's success.

Strategic implementation, the counterpart to planning, involves bringing these plans to life. This stage is where effective project management, efficient resource allocation, and diligent performance monitoring come into play. It's about turning the strategic vision into actionable steps and tangible results. Success in this phase hinges on clear communication, strong leadership, and a culture that values adaptability and accountability. These elements are crucial for navigating the complexities and seizing the opportunities that arise during implementation.

AI can play a pivotal role in enhancing both strategic planning and implementation in nonprofits. In the planning phase, AI can offer deep insights through data analysis. By processing historical data, current trends, and predictive modeling, AI tools can help identify opportunities and foresee potential challenges, allowing for more informed and strategic decision making. AI can analyze patterns in donor behavior, community needs, and market dynamics, providing a data-driven foundation for the strategic plan.

In the implementation phase, AI's contribution is equally significant. AI tools can assist in project management by optimizing resource allocation, tracking progress, and identifying areas where adjustments are needed. Additionally, AI can monitor the effectiveness of various initiatives, providing real-time feedback that can inform adjustments to operational plans.

Furthermore, AI can facilitate communication and engagement with stakeholders through personalized messages, automated updates, and interactive platforms that keep all parties informed and involved in the implementation process.

Utilizing AI as a strategic planning and implementation tool, nonprofit organizations can achieve a higher level of precision, efficiency, and effectiveness in their endeavors. AI not only supports the strategic process with data and analytics but also enhances the execution of these plans, ensuring that nonprofits can effectively work toward their mission and make a meaningful impact.

Resource Development

Resource development stands as a vital pillar in the structure of nonprofit management. It encompasses a wide array of activities aimed at securing the necessary resources—both financial and nonfinancial— for the smooth operation and success of the organization's programs. Effective resource development is not a monolithic task; it requires a diversified approach that includes tapping into individual and corporate donations, pursuing grants, soliciting in-kind contributions, and organizing fundraising events. Each of these streams plays a crucial role in ensuring a steady flow of resources.

Central to successful resource development is the ability to build and maintain robust relationships with donors and partners. This aspect of resource development calls for a high degree of transparency in operations, regular and meaningful communication, and a sincere acknowledgment and appreciation of contributions. In today's dynamic world, staying abreast of the evolving landscape of philanthropy is also vital. This includes understanding emerging fundraising technologies, adapting to changing donor preferences, and leveraging new platforms for donor engagement.

AI can significantly bolster efforts in resource development. AI technologies can help in analyzing donor data, enabling organizations to understand donor behavior and preferences better. This understanding can inform more personalized and effective donor engagement strategies, enhancing the likelihood of donations. AI can also identify patterns and trends in giving, which can be critical in planning and executing fundraising campaigns.

Moreover, AI-driven tools can streamline the process of identifying potential grant opportunities and corporate partnerships, matching the organization's needs with suitable funding sources. This can save considerable time and resources, allowing the nonprofit to focus more on its core mission.

In terms of donor management, AI can automate many aspects of communication and relationship management. From sending out personalized thank-you notes to providing regular updates on the impact of donations, AI can help maintain an active and engaging relationship with donors.

Additionally, AI can play a role in predicting future funding trends, helping organizations to proactively adapt their resource development strategies. This predictive capability can be crucial for long-term planning and sustainability.

Integrating AI into resource development offers nonprofits an opportunity to enhance their fundraising and donor engagement efforts, making them more effective, efficient, and aligned with contemporary trends in philanthropy. With AI, nonprofits can not only maintain their financial health but also ensure they are well-positioned to continue making a positive impact in their respective fields.

Financial Management

In the realm of nonprofit organizations, financial management serves as a crucial backbone, ensuring the judicious use and oversight of financial resources. It encompasses a broad spectrum of activities, including meticulous budgeting, accurate accounting, comprehensive financial reporting, and rigorous auditing. The essence of effective financial management in a nonprofit context lies in the ability to utilize funds efficiently, adhere strictly to financial rules and regulations, and sustain the confidence of donors and stakeholders through transparency and accountability.

A robust financial management system is characterized by strong internal controls and transparent financial practices. These systems are vital for accurately tracking and reporting both expenses and revenues, which is essential for maintaining the financial health of the organization. Additionally, financial management involves forecasting future financial needs and identifying potential risks. This foresight is indispensable for strategic decision making, as it ensures the organization is well-prepared to navigate future challenges and seize emerging opportunities, thereby securing its mission in the long term.

AI can play a transformative role in enhancing the financial management of nonprofit organizations. AI technologies offer advanced tools for financial analysis, enabling deeper insights into financial data. This can include automated tracking of income and expenditures, real-time budget monitoring, and predictive analysis for financial planning. These capabilities allow for more accurate and timely financial decision making.

AI can assist in risk assessment by identifying potential financial pitfalls before they become critical issues. It can analyze market trends and financial data to forecast potential changes in funding sources, donor behaviors, or economic conditions that might impact the organization's finances. This predictive capacity is invaluable in strategic financial planning.

AI-driven tools can also streamline financial reporting processes, ensuring compliance with regulatory requirements and enhancing the accuracy and reliability of financial statements. Automated financial reporting reduces the likelihood of human error and frees up valuable resources to focus on strategic financial planning and analysis.

In internal controls and auditing, AI can detect anomalies and potential areas of concern, providing an additional layer of scrutiny that bolsters the organization's financial integrity.

Integrating AI into financial management processes offers nonprofits an opportunity to manage their financial resources more effectively and strategically. This integration not only improves operational efficiency but also plays a crucial role in ensuring the organization's financial sustainability and its ability to fulfill its mission effectively.

Program Development and Project Management

Program development is central to the mission of any nonprofit, involving the creation and implementation of initiatives designed to meet specific community needs or achieve organizational goals. This crucial process starts with comprehensive research to gain an in-depth understanding of the target population's needs, evaluate the efficacy of current programs, and identify any service gaps. Meticulous planning and research lay the foundation for programs that are both relevant and impactful.

Once a program has been thoroughly conceptualized, the focus shifts to project management—the vital process of bringing these ideas to life. Effective project management in the nonprofit sector encompasses a wide range of activities, including meticulous planning, execution, ongoing monitoring, and the eventual closing of projects. It's a cycle that ensures projects not only adhere to their timelines and budgets but also achieve their intended outcomes. Moreover, this process involves continuous evaluation and adjustment based on feedback, ensuring that programs remain effective and in line with the evolving needs of the community.

Both program development and project management in nonprofits necessitate a collaborative and inclusive approach. This involves engaging various stakeholders, staff, and volunteers, ensuring that the programs are not only effective and responsive but also resonant with the values and mission of the organization.

In the program development phase, AI can analyze large volumes of data from various sources including community surveys, demographic studies, and feedback from past initiatives to identify trends and insights. These insights can inform the development of more targeted and effective programs.

In project management, AI tools can assist in various aspects, from scheduling and resource allocation to progress tracking and risk management. AI systems can provide real-time updates on the project's status, highlight potential bottlenecks, and suggest adjustments to keep projects on track. They can also help in predictive analysis, forecasting potential challenges and their impact on the project's timeline and deliverables.

Additionally, AI can play a crucial role in evaluating the impact of programs. By processing data from project reports and feedback mechanisms, AI can quantify the effectiveness of programs, offering a data-driven approach to impact assessment. This not only aids in reporting and accountability but also provides valuable insights for future program development and strategic decision making.

In summary, the integration of AI into program development and project management can greatly improve the efficiency and effectiveness of these processes. By leveraging AI's capabilities in data analysis, predictive modeling, and process optimization, nonprofits can ensure that their programs are not only well-planned and managed but also align with their mission and make a meaningful impact.

Stakeholder Management, Marketing, and Communication

For nonprofits to thrive and effectively fulfill their missions, understanding and managing relationships with a diverse range of stakeholders is crucial. Stakeholder management in the nonprofit sector is a dynamic process that includes identifying and comprehending the diverse needs and expectations of various groups such as donors, volunteers, beneficiaries, community members, and partners. This process is central to ensuring that the organization's activities and goals are aligned with the interests and needs of those they serve and those who support them.

Effective communication and marketing are integral to successful stakeholder management. Nonprofits must adeptly communicate their mission, goals, and the impact of their work to a broad audience. This communication strategy often encompasses a mix of traditional marketing materials and modern digital media platforms, catering to a wide range of stakeholders with varying preferences. Effective communication not only aids in building brand awareness and garnering support but is also essential in establishing and maintaining trust and transparency with all stakeholders.

Engaging stakeholders in meaningful ways is another key aspect. This can include incorporating feedback mechanisms to gather insights, providing volunteer opportunities that foster a deeper connection with the organization, or initiating collaborative projects that bring stakeholders closer to the nonprofit's mission and activities.

AI tools can analyze stakeholder data to gain insights into preferences and behaviors, enabling personalized communication strategies. For instance, AI can help segment donors based on their donation history and engagement levels, allowing for targeted communication and engagement strategies.

In marketing, AI can optimize digital marketing efforts through predictive analytics, helping nonprofits understand which content resonates best with their audience and when is the optimal time to disseminate it. AI-driven analytics can also measure the impact of different marketing strategies, providing valuable feedback for continuous improvement.

AI can even facilitate more effective stakeholder engagement. Chatbots and AI-driven interfaces can provide stakeholders with immediate responses and information, enhancing their experience and engagement with the nonprofit. AI can also process feedback from various channels, providing nonprofits with a comprehensive understanding of stakeholder sentiments and needs.

Integrating AI into stakeholder management, marketing, and communication processes can lead to more personalized, efficient, and impactful interactions with stakeholders. This integration not only strengthens relationships but also ensures that nonprofits can effectively convey their mission and impact, fostering a supportive community around their cause.

Human Resource Management

In the nonprofit sector, HRM plays a critical role in harnessing the potential of the organization's most valuable asset—its people. HRM in this context involves a spectrum of activities, including the recruitment, onboarding, training, performance management, and retention of both staff and volunteers. Given the often limited resources in nonprofits, HRM demands innovative and thoughtful strategies to attract, nurture, and retain talented individuals who are not only skilled but also align with the organization's mission and values.

This challenge often involves creating compelling nonmonetary incentives, such as opportunities for professional development, flexible working conditions, and fostering a workplace culture that resonates with the motivations of employees and volunteers. These strategies are vital in building a workforce that is not only competent but also deeply committed to the organization's goals.

Effective HRM is instrumental in driving employee engagement and productivity. It ensures that the staff and volunteers are well-equipped, motivated, and aligned with the nonprofit's objectives. This alignment is crucial, as it directly influences the organization's efficacy in achieving its mission.

AI can significantly contribute to enhancing HRM in nonprofits. AI-driven tools can streamline various HR processes, from recruitment to performance management. For instance, AI can assist in the recruitment process by analyzing resumes and application materials to identify candidates who best match the job requirements and organizational culture. This not only saves time but also ensures a more objective and efficient screening process.

In terms of training and development, AI can offer personalized learning experiences for employees and volunteers. By analyzing individual learning styles and progress, AI can suggest tailored training programs, enhancing the effectiveness of professional development efforts.

Performance management is another area where AI can make a substantial impact. AI tools can track performance metrics, provide insights for employee development, and identify areas where support is needed. This can lead to more informed and constructive performance evaluations, helping staff and volunteers grow and succeed in their roles.

Additionally, AI can play a pivotal role in bolstering employee engagement and retention initiatives. Utilizing AI to sift through employee feedback and satisfaction surveys, organizations can uncover underlying patterns and pinpoint specific areas needing attention within the workplace environment. This data-driven approach empowers management to make informed decisions aimed at fostering a more positive and nurturing work culture.

To encapsulate, the adoption of AI within HRM practices offers a substantial enhancement in managing a nonprofit's human resources with greater efficiency and efficacy. Employing AI across various HR facets, from the recruitment process to ongoing performance management, enables nonprofits to refine their HR operations. This, in turn, leads to the cultivation of a workforce that is not only more engaged and productive but also more aligned with the organization's core mission, significantly aiding in achieving long-term organizational success and durability.

Next...

In the chapters that follow, we will embark on a detailed exploration of each of the seven fundamental management functions, crucial for the successful operation of nonprofit organizations. This book is designed to serve as an introductory guide, providing insights and sparking innovative ideas, particularly in the application of AI within the nonprofit sector. However, the true essence and innovative potential of these ideas will be fully realized by the millions of dedicated nonprofit professionals around the world. As these individuals delve into the concepts presented, they will undoubtedly discover new and inventive ways to harness AI, adapting this technology to meet the specific needs and challenges of their organizations.

The dynamic nature of the nonprofit sector, coupled with the transformative capabilities of AI, opens up a myriad of possibilities. From improving donor engagement and resource allocation to enhancing program delivery and impact assessment, the potential applications of AI are vast and varied. As nonprofit professionals experiment with and implement AI-driven solutions, we anticipate witnessing a significant evolution in how nonprofits operate and achieve their missions.

Our discussions in this book aim to encourage and inspire this exploration. By offering a baseline understanding of both management principles and AI's capabilities, we hope to ignite a curiosity and drive for innovation among nonprofit leaders and staff. This exploration is not just about the adoption of new technology; it's about rethinking traditional approaches, challenging existing paradigms, and embracing the opportunities that AI presents for greater efficiency, effectiveness, and impact in the nonprofit world. The journey of integrating AI into nonprofit management is one of continuous learning, adaptation, and growth, and it holds the promise of profoundly transforming the sector for the better.

CHAPTER 5

Governance

Leadership is the capacity to translate vision into reality.[1]

—**Warren Bennis**

In the intricate tapestry of nonprofit organizations, governance stands as a crucial thread that weaves together the fabric of purpose, action, and accountability. It is in this space that the essence of leadership—as articulated by Warren Bennis, "Leadership is the capacity to translate vision into reality"—finds its most profound expression. Effective governance in nonprofit organizations is more than just a set of policies or a framework of operations; it is the embodiment of leadership that transforms visionary ideas into tangible outcomes that benefit communities and causes.

At the heart of nonprofit governance is the board of directors or trustees, a team that bears the responsibility of steering the organization toward its mission while upholding the values and ethics that define it. These leaders are tasked with a delicate balancing act: they must ensure the organization's integrity and effectiveness while navigating the complex and often challenging landscape of nonprofit management.

A compelling vision within a nonprofit organization serves as a powerful magnet, attracting and energizing individuals who share the same passions and values. When a board of directors articulates a clear, inspiring vision, it does more than just set a direction; it actively engages and motivates others to act. This vision becomes a rallying point, a beacon that draws in volunteers, staff, donors, and community members, uniting them under a common goal. It's the board's responsibility to not only define and communicate this vision but also to embody and champion it in every aspect of the organization's operations. By doing so, they create a sense of shared purpose and commitment, turning the vision into a collective endeavor where each person feels connected and vital to the cause. This ability to attract and mobilize a community around a shared vision is one of the most powerful tools a nonprofit board has, transforming their vision from a mere idea into a dynamic force for change and impact.

In translating vision into reality, these leaders must be adept at strategic planning, understanding the needs of those they serve, and making decisions that align with the organization's goals. They must foster an environment of transparency and accountability, ensuring that every action and decision taken is in the best interest of the mission and the community. The governance of nonprofit organizations is a manifestation of leadership in its most impactful form. It is about bringing to life the vision that sparked the organization's creation, navigating through challenges, and ultimately making a difference in the world.

Governance in the nonprofit sector is continually evolving. It requires leaders who are not only committed to the cause but are also responsive to the changing dynamics of the sector, including technological advancements, shifting donor expectations, and regulatory changes. These leaders must be innovators and adapters, capable of guiding their organizations through growth and change while staying true to their core mission.

Two Dimensions of Governance

In the journey of transforming a vision into action, governance in the nonprofit sector is anchored by two crucial aspects. First, there is the critical task of building a professional and effective governance structure. This foundation lays the groundwork for everything the organization does. It involves assembling a board of directors with diverse skills and perspectives, creating clear policies and procedures, and establishing robust systems for oversight and decision making. This structure must not only align with the organization's mission and values but also be flexible enough to adapt to changing circumstances and challenges.

The second aspect is the successful operation of this governance structure. It's not enough to simply have a well-designed framework; the true measure of its effectiveness lies in how it is put into practice. This includes regular and meaningful board meetings, active participation of board members in strategic planning and monitoring, transparent and ethical decision-making processes, and effective communication channels both within the board and with the organization's stakeholders. Operating a governance structure successfully means that the board doesn't just oversee the organization's work; it actively contributes to its strategic direction and growth.

Together, these two aspects form the bedrock of effective governance. While the first provides the necessary framework and tools, the second breathes life into the vision, ensuring that the organization not only sets goals but achieves them, thereby making a tangible impact in the communities it serves.

Drawing from our extensive experience working with a myriad of nonprofit organizations, we've witnessed a diverse spectrum of

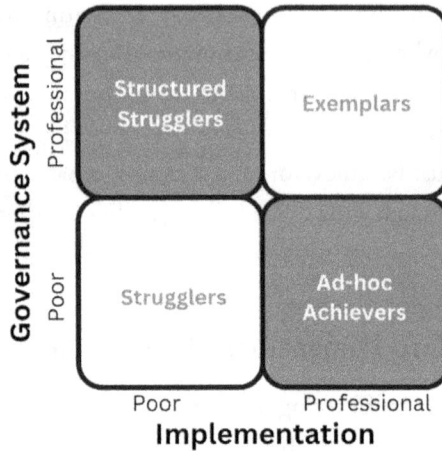

Figure 5.1 Governance system versus implementation

governance scenarios. Our observations reveal four distinct cases as illustrated in Figure 5.1 each highlighting the complex interplay between governance structures and their execution.

In some instances, we've encountered organizations equipped with robust governance frameworks that, regrettably, falter in effective implementation. We call them structured strugglers. These organizations possess all the necessary elements for success—comprehensive policies, clearly defined roles, and structured procedures. However, they struggle to translate these theoretical frameworks into practical, impactful action. This gap often stems from challenges such as limited resources, insufficient engagement from board members, or operational hurdles, preventing the governance structure from reaching its full potential.

A typical *structured struggler* might be an organization like a regional environmental advocacy group that has a solid board structure and clear governance policies but faces challenges in effectively implementing these strategies. Despite their well-defined governance framework, they might struggle with engaging their board members in active decision-making or translating policies into daily operations.

On the other hand, we've seen organizations that demonstrate commendable governance practices despite having less formalized structures. We call them ad hoc achievers. These entities often operate effectively due to strong leadership, a culture of adaptability, and a deep commitment from their team. While they may lack stringent formal structures, their practical approach and agility enable them to navigate various challenges successfully. However, the lack of formalization can sometimes pose risks to their long-term sustainability and ability to scale.

An *ad-hoc achiever* could be exemplified by a grassroots arts education nonprofit that operates without a formalized governance structure but is highly effective in its mission delivery. They might rely on a small, committed team and community volunteers, operating with flexibility and adaptability, yet delivering impactful arts programs successfully without a formal governance framework.

There are also those organizations where both the governance structure and practices are lacking. They are strugglers. These cases typically signify a fundamental need for development in governance, encompassing clearer strategic direction, stronger leadership, better allocation of resources, and more defined operational processes.

An example of a *struggler* organization could be a newly formed nonprofit like a local community aid group that has emerged in response to an immediate need, such as a natural disaster. Such organizations often start with a strong mission but struggle to develop structured governance and operational processes due to their rapid formation and limited experience.

In the most ideal situations, we've observed organizations that exhibit successful governance underpinned by strong, well-established structures: governance exemplars. These nonprofits stand as exemplary models, combining solid, well-defined governance frameworks with effective practical implementation. They benefit from engaged and committed leadership, clear strategic directives, robust accountability measures, and active involvement from all stakeholders, all contributing to their substantial impact and success.

An example of a *governance exemplar* is an organization like the Wikimedia Foundation, the nonprofit behind Wikipedia. They demonstrate a robust governance structure with clear policies, active board involvement, and transparent operations, coupled with effective implementation of their strategies. This strong governance enables them to manage global operations successfully, ensuring their mission's sustainability and impact.

Through our experiences, one key lesson becomes evident: effective governance in the nonprofit sector is a harmonious blend of structured framework and practical application. It involves establishing the right foundation and dedicating the necessary commitment and resources to bring it to fruition. Each organization's path to achieving this ideal balance may vary, but the objective remains consistent—to forge governance that is as impactful and effective as the mission it supports.

How Can AI Help?

In the diverse landscape of nonprofit governance, each type faces unique challenges and opportunities in their pursuit of effective governance and operational success. AI presents itself as a transformative tool across these categories, offering tailored solutions that range from establishing foundational governance structures to enhancing operational efficiency and strategic decision making. In this section, we explore how AI can be a pivotal asset to each of these governance types, aiding them in overcoming their specific challenges and capitalizing on their strengths to maximize their impact.

Strugglers

For organizations categorized as strugglers, which face foundational challenges in both structure and governance practices, AI offers a beacon of hope. It can be instrumental in laying down the ground-work for effective governance. AI-driven tools can help in mapping out efficient operational processes, identifying areas where resources can be optimized, and providing templates for basic governance structures such as by-laws, and policy documents. Additionally, AI's ability to analyze large data sets can help these organizations understand their operational environment better and make more informed decisions, setting a stronger foundation for future growth and development.

Structured Strugglers

Organizations in the *structured strugglers* category have established governance frameworks but struggle with implementation. Here, AI can be a game-changer in operationalizing these structures. By automating administrative tasks and streamlining processes, AI allows staff to focus more on strategic objectives rather than day-to-day tasks. Moreover, AI analytics can play a pivotal role in monitoring the effectiveness of governance practices and providing insights for improvement, helping these organizations to bridge the gap between their well-laid plans and their execution.

Ad Hoc Achievers

Ad hoc achievers, though they lack formal structures, excel through adaptability and responsiveness. AI can augment these strengths by providing real-time data analysis and predictive insights, aiding these organizations in making quick and informed decisions. AI can also help in formalizing some of their processes without compromising their agility, providing a balance between structure and flexibility. This could involve using AI for targeted donor outreach, program evaluation, or even optimizing resource allocation, thereby enhancing their operational efficiency while maintaining their adaptive edge.

Governance Exemplars

For governance exemplars, which exhibit an ideal blend of strong governance structures and effective practices, AI can act as a tool for continuous improvement and innovation. These organizations can use AI for advanced data analysis to refine their strategies, explore new opportunities for impact, and stay ahead of emerging trends in the nonprofit sector. AI can also assist in scaling their successful models, enabling them to expand their reach and impact while maintaining governance excellence.

In each of these cases, AI serves as a powerful ally, helping nonprofits at various stages of governance maturity to optimize their operations, make data-driven decisions, and ultimately enhance their impact and sustainability.

Defining the Mission

If you're serving on the board of a nonprofit organization, let's begin with a simple exercise. Without referring to any documents, try to recall your organization's mission statement. What words and phrases come to mind? Now, take a moment to compare your recollection with the actual mission statement as it appears on your organization's website. Do they match? Chances are, they don't align perfectly, and that's quite normal. But don't stop there; conduct this exercise with your fellow board members. You might be surprised to discover the variations in how each member perceives and remembers the mission statement. This disparity is a common phenomenon but one that highlights a crucial area for alignment within the organization. It's a revealing test that can often shed light on the coherence and unity of the board concerning the core purpose and direction of your nonprofit.

Clarifying the mission of a nonprofit, particularly when resources are limited, is a critical task that necessitates focus and strategic planning. Based on our experience, nonprofit board members often bring a wealth of passion and innovation to the table. Their drive to help and make a difference frequently leads to a plethora of ideas and potential projects. While this enthusiasm is invaluable, it can also pose a challenge. Without a focused approach, the risk of spreading resources too thinly over a wide array of projects can dilute the organization's impact and strain its sustainability.

The key lies in honing in on what truly matters. This involves taking a step back to assess the core mission and identifying the areas where the organization can make the most significant impact. It's about quality over quantity, concentrating efforts and resources on specific tasks or projects that align closely with the organization's goals and have the potential for the greatest impact. This focused approach not only maximizes the effectiveness of each initiative but also ensures that the organization's limited resources are utilized in the most efficient and impactful manner.

AI can play a pivotal role in this process of clarifying and focusing the mission. AI can assist in analyzing data to identify the most pressing needs within the community or sector the nonprofit serves. It can provide insights into where the organization's efforts might be most needed and where they can achieve the most substantial outcomes. Additionally, AI can help in evaluating the success of past and current projects, offering data-driven feedback on their impact and effectiveness. This analysis can guide decision making, helping to prioritize projects that align with the core mission and have a proven track record of success.

Our ViStA Strategic Management Framework, with its emphasis on the perfect alignment between vision, mission, strategies, and operations, serves as a critical tool in ensuring the coherence and effectiveness of nonprofit organizations. At the core of this framework is the strategic evaluation process, which begins with a review of the nonprofit's mission statement. This step is foundational, as the mission statement guides the organization's direction and decision making.

However, in practice, our experience has shown a surprising and common challenge during sessions with nonprofit boards: a lack of unanimous understanding or recollection of the organization's mission statement. Board members often struggle to recall the exact wording of the mission statement as it appears in their bylaws or on their website. More concerning is the frequent occurrence of differing interpretations of the mission among board members. This discrepancy is not just a matter of forgetfulness but signifies a deeper issue of misalignment within the organization.

Such misalignment at the mission level can have cascading effects on the entire strategic management process. If the board members, who are responsible for steering the organization, are not on the same page regarding the fundamental purpose of their work, it becomes challenging to develop cohesive and effective strategies. This disconnect can extend to operational decisions, leading to inefficiencies and a dilution of the organization's impact.

The resolution of this issue is crucial for the health and success of a nonprofit. It necessitates a concerted effort to not only revisit and reaffirm the mission statement but also to ensure that every board member understands and internalizes it. This alignment at the top level is essential for the successful implementation of the ViStA Strategic Management Framework, as it ensures that every strategy and operational decision made is in service of a commonly understood and shared mission. Only then can a nonprofit expect to achieve clarity in its direction and effectiveness in its operations.

The issue of divergent priorities among board members is a common challenge in nonprofits, particularly when it comes to crafting a shared mission statement. Each member brings their unique perspective and priorities, which, while valuable, can make it difficult to find a common ground. In such situations, leveraging tools like ChatGPT can be highly beneficial.

Use AI to compile and synthesize the different ideas and priorities expressed by board members. By inputting all the relevant information—including key objectives, values, and the vision of each board member—you can ask the AI to suggest a draft mission statement. This AI-generated statement can serve as a strong baseline for further discussions. It offers a consolidated view of the diverse inputs, ensuring that all perspectives are considered.

While the AI-suggested mission statement might not be the final version you adopt, it functions as an effective starting point. It can significantly streamline the process, quickly bringing you to a cohesive and representative mission statement draft. This approach not only saves time but also facilitates a more structured and efficient discussion among board members, guiding you toward a mission statement that truly reflects the collective vision and goals of your organization.

AI: Aiding, Not Replacing, Decision Makers in Nonprofit Boards

In the realm of nonprofit governance, AI emerges not as a tool for making decisions but as a robust system supporting those decisions. Understanding how to leverage AI effectively can significantly enhance the board's capacity to make informed, strategic decisions.

AI can be an invaluable ally in processing vast amounts of data—from donor trends and community needs assessments to operational metrics. This data, which might be overwhelming to analyze manually, can be quickly processed by AI, providing the board with concise, actionable insights. For instance, AI can identify patterns in donor behavior, predict fundraising success based on historical data, or even suggest areas where operational efficiency can be improved. These insights allow the board to make decisions that are data-driven and aligned with the organization's goals and needs.

Moreover, AI can assist in scenario planning and risk assessment. By simulating different strategies and their potential outcomes, the board can better understand the implications of their decisions. This is particularly useful in strategic planning, where the consequences of each choice can significantly impact the organization's direction and success.

However, it's crucial for board members to remember that AI is a tool to aid, not replace, human judgment. The final decision-making responsibility rests with the board, which must consider not only the data but also the organization's values, mission, and the ethical implications of their choices. AI provides a powerful lens through which to view information, but the interpretation and application of this information require human oversight and intuition.

For a nonprofit board, AI offers a way to navigate the complexities of decision making in today's data-rich world. By using AI as a decision support system, boards can enhance their strategic planning, operational efficiency, and overall effectiveness, leading to better outcomes for their organizations and the communities they serve.

Utilizing AI in Advocacy and Policy Development

In the dynamic world of nonprofit advocacy and policy development, AI is emerging as a key player. By leveraging AI, organizations can enhance their advocacy efforts, making them more targeted and impactful. AI algorithms can analyze large datasets, including public opinions gathered from social media, forums, and surveys, providing insights into the issues that resonate most with the community and stakeholders. This data-driven approach allows nonprofits to tailor their advocacy campaigns more effectively, ensuring that they address the most pressing concerns and engage with the right audience.

Additionally, AI can play a significant role in policy development. By processing and synthesizing vast amounts of information related to public policy and legislation, AI can help identify trends, forecast policy outcomes, and even predict the impact of certain policy changes. This enables organizations to formulate well-informed policy recommendations and strategic plans that align with both their mission and current socio-political landscapes.

Financial Oversight and Impact Assessment

AI's potential extends into the critical board functions of financial oversight and impact assessment. In the realm of financial oversight, AI tools can analyze financial transactions, budgets, and funding patterns, providing real-time insights into the financial health of the organization. This level of analysis helps in identifying areas of financial risks, potential inefficiencies, and opportunities for cost savings. AI-driven financial analytics supports the board in making more informed decisions regarding resource allocation, investments, and fundraising strategies.

When it comes to impact assessment and monitoring, AI can transform how nonprofits measure and understand the effects of their work. By analyzing data from various sources, including project reports, beneficiary feedback, and community surveys, AI can help quantify the impact of the organization's programs. This not only aids in reporting and accountability but also guides the board in strategic decision making. Organizations can use these insights to refine their programs, enhance their effectiveness, and better communicate their impact to donors, stakeholders, and the public.

Adding to the critical functions of AI in financial oversight and impact assessment, another remarkable capability of AI lies in monitoring the macroeconomic environment. This feature can significantly enhance a nonprofit board's ability to make well-informed, forward-looking decisions.

AI's advanced analytics and machine learning algorithms can process and interpret vast arrays of macroeconomic data—from global market trends and economic forecasts to regulatory changes and demographic shifts. This analysis provides a comprehensive view of the external economic factors that could impact the nonprofit's operations and financial stability. Unlike traditional methods, AI can continuously monitor these macroeconomic variables, providing real-time updates and predictions that are more accurate and detailed than those a human economist could feasibly compile.

Moreover, AI's predictive capabilities extend beyond current trends to forecast future economic scenarios. By analyzing historical data and current market signals, AI can predict potential economic downturns, shifts in donor behavior, or changes in funding landscapes. This foresight allows nonprofit boards to proactively adjust their strategies, whether it's diversifying funding sources, modifying budget allocations, or reorienting programs to better align with the predicted economic conditions.

Incorporating AI's macroeconomic monitoring and predictive analysis into their strategic planning enables nonprofits to be more agile and resilient. It supports the board in navigating economic uncertainties and making decisions that safeguard the organization's financial health and ensure the continuity of its impact. In essence, AI acts as a sophisticated economic advisor, providing insights that are crucial for strategic financial planning and long-term sustainability in the ever-changing economic landscape.

Fostering Diversity in Nonprofit Boards

The composition of a nonprofit board is pivotal in shaping the organization's direction, effectiveness, and inclusivity. Embracing diversity, both in terms of ethnocultural backgrounds and professional skills, is key to forming a board that is not only representative of the community it serves but also rich in perspectives and expertise.

Diversity in ethnocultural backgrounds on a nonprofit board ensures a wide range of viewpoints, reflective of a multifaceted society. This variety fosters an environment where different cultural insights and experiences contribute to more empathetic and comprehensive decision making. A board that mirrors the diversity of the community enhances the organization's ability to connect with and understand the needs of its constituents, leading to more effective and culturally sensitive program development.

On the other hand, diversity in professional skills is equally crucial. A board with a mix of expertise—from financial and legal professionals to educators, health care professionals, and technology experts—can approach challenges from various angles. This multidisciplinary approach enables the board to tackle complex issues more effectively and fosters innovative solutions. For instance, a tech professional can bring insights into digital transformation and AI integration, while a financial expert can offer guidance on budgeting and financial sustainability.

However, achieving this diversity goes beyond just recruitment. It involves creating an inclusive environment where all board members feel valued and empowered to share their perspectives. Regular training and development opportunities should be provided to ensure that board members are equipped to contribute effectively. Additionally, the board should continually assess its composition and seek ways to enhance its diversity, ensuring it evolves with changing societal dynamics.

A diverse board is a strong board. By embracing both ethnocultural and professional diversity, nonprofit organizations can ensure more robust governance, deeper community connections, and more impactful and sustainable outcomes.

AI can even play a transformative role in the recruitment process for nonprofit boards, particularly in identifying and engaging potential candidates. By utilizing AI, nonprofits can streamline and enhance the efficiency and effectiveness of their board recruitment efforts.

AI algorithms can scan through vast databases to identify potential candidates within a city or neighborhood who align with the organization's needs and values. This process includes analyzing public profiles, professional networks, and databases to find individuals with the desired ethnocultural backgrounds, professional skills, and experience relevant to the nonprofit's mission. AI can evaluate these factors against the organization's specific requirements, ensuring a more targeted and strategic approach to candidate selection.

Moreover, AI can be programmed to initiate preliminary conversations with potential candidates. For instance, AI-driven chatbots can reach out to identified individuals, providing information about the organization and its board opportunities, and gauging their interest and suitability. This not only saves time and resources but also ensures that the outreach process is consistent and far-reaching.

However, it's important to note that while AI can significantly aid the recruitment process, the final decision making should involve human judgment and interaction. AI can bring candidates to the table, but the nuances of personal interactions, alignment of values, and mutual understanding are aspects that are best assessed through direct human engagement.

Leveraging AI for board recruitment will offer nonprofits a powerful tool to identify and engage diverse and qualified board members efficiently. It will enhance the recruitment process, ensuring that the organization can build a strong, diverse, and effective board to guide its mission and impact.

CHAPTER 6

Strategic Planning and Implementation

Strategy without tactics is the slowest route to victory. Tactics without strategy is the noise before defeat.[1]

—**Sun Tzu**

Sun Tzu's timeless principle, "Strategy without tactics is the slowest route to victory. Tactics without strategy is the noise before defeat,"

bears significant relevance for nonprofit organizations, particularly in the application of AI. This concept emphasizes the critical importance of harmonizing overarching plans (strategy) with actionable measures (tactics), especially within the context of leveraging AI. For non-profits aiming to address grand challenges, such as combating poverty, enhancing educational outcomes, or preserving the environment, developing a comprehensive strategy is paramount. AI could play a crucial role in this process by analyzing extensive datasets to identify optimal approaches and predict potential impacts.

Yet, a strategy without actionable steps, informed and augmented by AI, may lead to minimal progress in achieving the organization's mission. AI's capability to facilitate targeted interventions, automate routine tasks, and personalize interactions ensures that each effort contributes effectively toward the strategic objectives.

Conversely, nonprofits that embark on tactical initiatives using AI without a cohesive overarching strategy might find themselves engaged in a flurry of activities that, despite being technologically advanced, lack purpose and direction. This approach, driven by AI without strategic guidance, can result in inefficiency and misalignment with the organization's core mission. Therefore, it is strongly advised for nonprofits to intricately weave their strategic visions with AI-powered operational tactics. Such an integration guarantees that every technologically enhanced action is a deliberate step toward fulfilling meaningful, strategically aligned objectives, underscoring the essential synergy between strategy, tactics, and technology in advancing social good.

AI to Develop Actionable Strategic Plans

When considering whether a strategic plan is necessary, integrating AI into the equation can shift the perspective significantly. The question often elicits a conditional *no*, assuming a scenario where an organization's leader has a perfect understanding of their goals, access to unlimited resources, and a comprehensive grasp of their operational environment. In such a utopian scenario, akin to driving a familiar route home without the need for GPS, the strategic goals and methods to achieve them are already clear, functioning as an internal strategic plan.

However, this ideal is far from the reality faced by most nonprofit organizations, where navigating the organization's direction is more like exploring an unfamiliar city. Without AI as a strategic planning tool, organizations risk getting lost or diverted from their mission. In this context, AI can act as a sophisticated navigation system, offering more than just directions; it provides insights, forecasts, and recommendations that can significantly enhance strategic planning processes. It would align efforts and decisions, ensuring that each taken step is in service of efficiently reaching the desired outcome. Therefore, in the constantly evolving nonprofit sector, characterized by changing priorities and limited resources, AI should become indispensable in crafting and guiding strategic plans toward achieving organizational goals.

Even when a strategic plan is not explicitly documented, it might still exist implicitly, especially within the leadership of startup nonprofits. Leaders often have a mental map of the organization's strategic direction, similar to navigating a well-known route without a GPS. However, as the organization grows and the operational landscape becomes more complex, the need for a formal, AI-enhanced strategic plan becomes evident. AI's ability to analyze data, identify patterns, and predict outcomes can make the strategic planning process more dynamic and informed. It can transform implicit strategies into documented plans that are not static but adaptive, evolving with the organization's needs and external changes.

Incorporating AI into strategic planning won't merely add a technological layer; it would revolutionize the way strategic plans are developed and implemented. AI can enable organizations to transition from implicit, mental maps of strategy to formal, actionable plans that are data-driven and goal-oriented. It can ensure that strategic planning is not just about documenting intentions but about creating a living, breathing blueprint for the organization's future. This blueprint is continuously informed by data and AI insights, making it an essential tool for guiding nonprofit organizations through their growth and helping them adapt to the complexities of their missions. AI, therefore, is not just an addition to the strategic planning toolkit; it is a fundamental shift in how strategic plans can be conceived, developed, and executed, ensuring that they are as effective and impactful as possible.

Incorporating AI into the strategic planning process can enhance each characteristic of a successful plan, exemplified by the acronym SEARCH (Simple, Effective, Actionable, Realistic, Comprehensive, Harmonized) as illustrated in Figure 6.1. This approach not only integrates technology into strategic planning but also ensures that each aspect of the plan is optimized for the unique challenges and opportunities faced by organizations today.

Simple: AI can simplify strategic planning by analyzing complex data sets and presenting insights in an understandable format. By leveraging AI, organizations can distill vast amounts of information into clear, actionable strategies. This use of AI helps maintain clarity in the strategic plan, ensuring that the direction and purpose are straightforward for all stakeholders to comprehend.

Effective: AI can enhance the effectiveness of strategic plans by providing data-driven insights and forecasting outcomes. By analyzing past performance and current trends, AI can identify strategies with a high likelihood of success. This capability allows organizations to base their plans on sound reasoning and predictive analytics, increasing the chances of achieving desired outcomes.

Actionable: With AI, strategic plans can become more actionable. AI tools can break down overarching strategies into specific, concrete steps by analyzing the required actions and resources. This process helps organizations translate their strategic visions into practical, implementable actions, facilitating a seamless transition from theory to practice.

Realistic: AI can contribute to creating realistic strategic plans by offering a detailed analysis of the organization's capabilities and external factors. Through AI-powered simulations and scenario planning, organizations can assess the feasibility of their goals and actions, ensuring they are achievable and practical within the given constraints and resources.

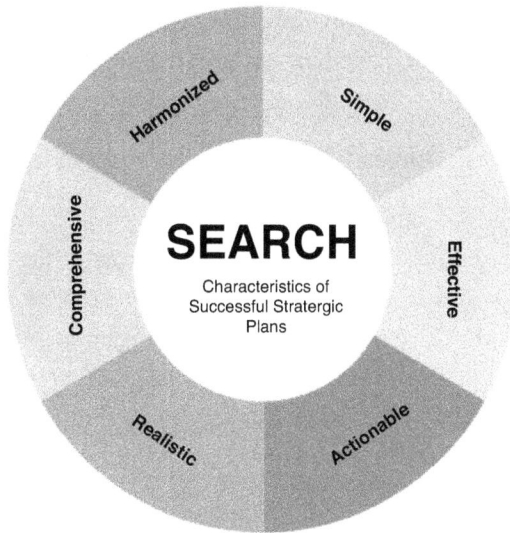

Figure 6.1 SEARCH characteristics

Comprehensive: AI can aid in developing comprehensive strategic plans by ensuring all critical areas of operation are covered. It can identify gaps in the plan and suggest areas that need attention, ensuring the plan addresses the needs of all stakeholders. By processing and analyzing data from various sources, AI helps create a thorough plan that leaves no critical aspect unaddressed.

Harmonized: Finally, AI can support the harmonization of strategies with the organization's mission, values, and culture. AI analytics can help identify alignment issues and ensure that the strategies proposed are in sync with the organization's core principles. This alignment is crucial for cohesive action across all levels and departments, promoting a unified approach to achieving the strategic goals.

By leveraging AI, organizations can ensure their strategic plans are not only designed with the SEARCH characteristics in mind but also enriched with insights and capabilities that only advanced technologies can provide. AI transforms strategic planning from a static, periodic exercise into a dynamic, ongoing process that continually adapts to new information and changing circumstances, positioning organizations for success in an increasingly complex and uncertain world.

Four Stages of Strategic Management

In the dynamic and rapidly evolving landscape of the nonprofit sector, strategic management, augmented by AI, emerges as the cornerstone for achieving sustainable success and impact. This process, now deeply intertwined with AI, systematically guides an organization through the assessment of its current position, the envisioning of its future, and the meticulous planning and execution of strategies to realize its objectives. The journey is segmented into four pivotal stages as shown in Figure 6.2.

Each of these stages is significantly enhanced by AI's capabilities, contributing uniquely to the organization's proactive navigation toward its mission. AI not only can streamline data analysis and strategic decision making but also can introduce predictive modeling and automation, bringing clarity, efficiency, and agility to each step of the strategic management process. Through AI, nonprofits can harness the power of advanced analytics, machine learning, and real-time data processing to adapt more swiftly to environmental changes, optimize operations, and maximize their impact.

Stage 1—Strategic Evaluation: Understanding Your Current Position and Future Goals

Imagine a nonprofit organization that aims to improve literacy rates in underserved communities. In its strategic evaluation phase, the organization decides to leverage AI to gain a comprehensive understanding of its current operations, resources, impact, and the communities it serves. Utilizing AI, the organization analyzes vast amounts of data from various sources, including targeted questionnaires filled out by board members, staff, volunteers, donors, and beneficiaries. This AI-driven process allows for the quantification and visualization of data, provid-

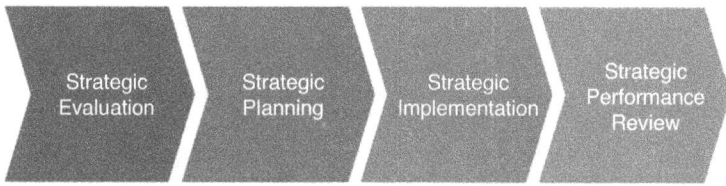

Strategic Evaluation → Strategic Planning → Strategic Implementation → Strategic Performance Review

Figure 6.2 Four stages of strategic management

ing a clear overview of the organization's current status and creating a baseline for measuring future progress.

The power of AI in this initial phase is transformative, offering depth in analysis and insights that were previously unattainable. By processing performance metrics, donor trends, and operational efficiencies, AI turns raw data into actionable insights. Moreover, AI's predictive analytics capabilities become a game-changer, enabling the nonprofit to forecast future trends and prepare for upcoming challenges and opportunities. This foresight is crucial for strategic decision making, allowing the organization to proactively adjust its strategies.

Further enhancing the strategic evaluation, AI delves into sentiment and perception analysis among stakeholders. Employing natural language processing, it analyzes feedback from social media and other communication channels to capture the sentiments of donors, beneficiaries, and staff accurately. This sentiment analysis offers a rich, comprehensive view of the organization's impact and community perception, providing valuable insights that enrich both the strategic evaluation and subsequent planning processes.

This AI-enhanced approach not only streamlines the strategic evaluation but also ensures that the strategies developed are informed by a thorough understanding of both the quantitative data and qualitative feedback from the organization's ecosystem. By integrating AI at this foundational stage, the nonprofit sets a solid groundwork for its future strategic planning, implementation, and review, aligning its efforts more closely with its mission and enhancing its potential for making a significant impact in the communities it serves.

Figure 6.3 ViSTA *strategic management framework*

Stage 2—Strategic Planning: Crafting a Roadmap for Success

Once the evaluation is complete, developing a strategic plan is next. This is where AI and the ViStA Strategic Management Framework comes into play. This framework guides in creating a comprehensive and actionable strategic plan, ensuring that every aspect of an organization's mission, vision, and operational capabilities is considered.

Consider a nonprofit dedicated to environmental conservation. As it embarks on strategic planning, it employs the ViStA Strategic Management Framework, as visualized in Figure 6.3, complemented by AI, to craft a roadmap for success. This approach begins with AI-driven scenario modeling, where the organization simulates various strategic paths using AI to project the outcomes of different initiatives under fluctuating environmental policies, funding levels, and community engagement rates. This predictive capability allows the nonprofit to visualize the potential impacts of its strategies, making well-informed, forward-looking decisions.

In this stage, AI becomes a pivotal asset, enhancing every facet of the strategic planning process. For resource optimization, AI algorithms evaluate past allocations and outcomes, identifying patterns and inefficiencies. This analysis helps the nonprofit pinpoint the most effective use of its resources, ensuring that financial, human, and material assets are leveraged to their fullest potential toward achieving the strategic objectives. This process not only streamlines resource allocation but also aligns it closely with the organization's long-term goals, making the strategic plan both visionary and pragmatic.

Moreover, AI significantly impacts goal setting and prioritization. By analyzing historical data and comparing it against industry benchmarks, AI tools offer insights into realistic and impactful goal formulation. This data-driven approach to setting objectives ensures they are ambitious yet attainable, tailored to the organization's strengths and the external market dynamics. It also facilitates a dynamic prioritization of goals, where AI's continuous learning capabilities can adjust priorities in response to new data or shifting contexts, keeping the strategic plan flexible and responsive.

This integration of AI into the strategic planning process ensures that the nonprofit's roadmap for success is not just a static document but a living strategy, adaptable to changing circumstances and enriched with insights from predictive analytics and resource optimization. The alignment achieved at the board level on this AI-enhanced strategic plan guarantees that every member of the organization is committed to the defined objectives, fully understanding their role in the collective effort to achieve them. Through AI, strategic planning evolves from a conventional exercise into a dynamic, data-informed process that positions the nonprofit for sustainable impact and growth.

Stage 3—Strategy Implementation: Making Your Plan a Reality

As a nonprofit organization gears up for the strategy implementation stage, it integrates AI from the outset to transform its strategic plan into actionable results. For instance, consider the organization deploying AI-driven project management tools to oversee the rollout of a new community health initiative. These tools not only schedule and track the progress of various tasks but also use predictive analytics to forecast potential bottlenecks and resource gaps. This proactive approach ensures that all resources, capabilities, and activities are precisely aligned with the strategic objectives, facilitating a smooth translation of plans into impactful actions.

During the implementation phase, the indispensability of AI becomes evident as it introduces unparalleled efficiency and agility into the process. AI-enhanced systems oversee project timelines and milestones, providing real-time updates and flagging any deviations from the plan. This level of detailed oversight is crucial for maintaining the momentum of strategic initiatives and promptly addressing challenges.

Moreover, AI plays a critical role in optimizing performance throughout the implementation phase. Through continuous analysis of operational data, AI algorithms identify areas for improvement, suggesting actionable optimizations. This capability allows for the strategy to be executed with the highest degree of effectiveness, ensuring resources are utilized optimally and initiatives are adjusted in real-time to meet evolving conditions and objectives.

The adaptability of strategy implementation is further enhanced by AI's ability to automate adjustments. AI systems can autonomously refine operational processes in response to external changes or internal performance feedback. This dynamic adjustment capability ensures that the strategic implementation remains relevant and impactful, even as the nonprofit navigates the complexities of its environment.

AI's contribution to strategy implementation thus extends beyond mere efficiency; it ensures that the strategic plan remains a living, breathing framework capable of adapting to new challenges and seizing opportunities as they arise. By leveraging AI, nonprofits can ensure that their strategic implementation is not just a series of tasks but a coherent, responsive journey toward achieving their mission, characterized by continuous learning and improvement.

Stage 4—Strategic Performance Review: Monitoring and Adapting

Imagine a nonprofit focused on global education initiatives, utilizing AI to revolutionize its strategic performance review phase. This organization employs AI tools to continuously track the progress of educational programs across different regions, comparing actual outcomes against the objectives set in its strategic plan. Through AI's advanced analytics, the nonprofit can assess the effectiveness of its strategies in real-time, identifying which programs are meeting or exceeding their goals and which require adjustments.

AI's role in reshaping the strategic performance review phase is critical, providing precise, insightful measurements of each initiative's impact. By aligning the outcomes with the strategic objectives and key performance indicators, AI offers an unambiguous view of the effectiveness of the organization's efforts. This clarity ensures that resources are allocated to initiatives that yield the best outcomes, optimizing the nonprofit's impact.

Furthermore, AI enables a data-driven approach to learning and adaptation. It analyzes the outcomes of various strategies, distinguishing between successful initiatives and those that fell short. This analysis not only highlights areas for improvement but also uncovers the factors contributing to success, providing valuable insights for future strategic planning. This iterative learning process ensures the organization remains agile, continuously refining its strategies based on solid data and real-world performance.

In terms of reporting and visualization, AI transforms how strategic performance insights are communicated to stakeholders. Automated reporting tools and dynamic dashboards, powered by AI, present complex data in an accessible and comprehensible format. This automation not only saves significant time but also enhances stakeholders' understanding of the nonprofit's progress, facilitating more informed discussions about future directions and strategies.

The transformative potential of AI in strategic management for nonprofits is profound. With its enhanced capabilities for data processing, predictive analytics, and decision support, AI equips nonprofits to navigate the complexities of their mission with unprecedented precision and adaptability. As nonprofits embrace AI in their strategic management processes, they are better positioned to plan, implement, and evolve their strategies effectively, ensuring they can achieve their goals and maximize their impact in an ever-changing global landscape. This evolution marks a significant milestone in strategic management, enabling nonprofits to not just respond to changes but to anticipate and prepare for them, securing their success and expanding their influence.

CHAPTER 7

Resource Development

It's not about having enough resources; it's about being resourceful with what you have.[1]

—**Tony Robbins**

In Ottawa, where we reside, the landscape is dotted with numerous outstanding charities devoted to tackling a range of social issues, from homelessness and poverty to racism and mental health challenges. Witnessing the dedication and commitment of these organizations, it's disheartening to observe the persistent gap between their ambitious goals and the limited budgets they operate within. Inspired by Tony Robbins' insight, "It's not about having enough resources; it's about being resourceful with what you have," these organizations are increasingly turning to AI as a means to bridge this divide. By harnessing AI, they embark on a transformative journey, optimizing their scarce funds, enhancing volunteer coordination, and streamlining their service offerings. This adaptation not only showcases their innovative spirit but also significantly amplifies their reach and impact within the community.

This narrative underscores a pivotal lesson for the nonprofit sector, not only in Ottawa but all around the world: the key to overcoming the challenges of limited resources lies not in the abundance of these resources but in the creative and efficient utilization of what is available. In an environment where constraints are a given, AI emerges as an essential tool for redefining resourcefulness. Local nonprofits leverage AI to decipher donation patterns, forecast resource requirements, and automate administrative processes, thereby maximizing the impact of every dollar, hour, and effort expended.

Incorporating AI into their operations amplifies these organizations' ability to be both innovative and efficient, enabling them to achieve impressive outcomes despite their resource limitations. Whether through optimizing donation allocations, streamlining operations, or making strategic decisions informed by data analytics, AI empowers these nonprofits to extend their resources further than ever before. This approach to resource development reflects Robbins' philosophy, highlighting that success hinges on maximizing the resources at hand. Through AI, nonprofits in Ottawa and beyond are turning the challenge of scarcity into an opportunity for innovation and growth, setting the stage for a more efficient, impactful, and resourceful future.

Seven Resource Categories

In the ecosystem of nonprofit organizations, the role of AI in amplifying and optimizing the use of primary resources (listed in Figure 7.1) cannot

Figure 7.1 Nonprofit resources

be overstated. AI stands as a pivotal force in transforming how these organizations operate, manage resources, and achieve their missions. Let's delve into how AI intersects with each key resource category, significantly enhancing efficiency and effectiveness:

Financial resources: AI can revolutionize fundraising and financial management. Through predictive analytics, nonprofits can identify potential donors and funding opportunities more effectively, tailor fundraising campaigns to specific audiences, and forecast financial trends to ensure stability and sustainability. AI-powered tools can also streamline donation processing and financial reporting, reducing administrative burdens and costs.

Human resources: AI can streamline recruitment by automating candidate screening, enhance training through personalized learning, and improve staff management with predictive analytics for performance optimization. By automating routine tasks, AI allows human resources to focus on strategic and impact-driven activities. Furthermore, AI-driven platforms can match volunteers' skills with the organization's needs, optimize scheduling, and facilitate remote collaboration, thus maximizing human capital.

Material resources: AI systems can improve inventory management and logistics, ensuring that material resources like food supplies, educational materials, or medical equipment are efficiently distributed and utilized. For example, AI can predict the demand for certain resources, optimize their allocation, and track their usage, reducing waste and increasing program effectiveness.

Informational resources: The power of AI to process and analyze vast amounts of data can revolutionize access to and the use of informational resources. AI tools can sift through research, data, and expert analyses to provide actionable insights, support evidence-based decision making, and enhance program development. Additionally, AI can help nonprofits navigate legal and professional landscapes by analyzing relevant documents and regulations.

Network and community resources: AI can facilitate the building and strengthening of networks by analyzing community needs, identifying potential partners, and suggesting collaboration opportunities. Social media algorithms and AI-driven communication tools can also help increase an organization's reach and engage more effectively with the community and stakeholders.

Technological resources: AI itself is a critical technological resource that enables nonprofits to adopt cutting-edge solutions for operation, communication, and service delivery. From Customer Relations management (CRM) systems powered by AI to enhance donor relationships, to AI-driven analytics platforms for monitoring and evaluation, the integration of AI tools ensures nonprofits remain at the forefront of technological innovation.

Time: Perhaps one of the most significant impacts of AI is on the optimization of time. By automating administrative tasks, streamlining processes, and enabling more efficient project management, AI frees up valuable time for strategic thinking, innovation, and focusing on mission-critical activities.

In sum, AI can act as a catalyst across all resource categories within nonprofit organizations, driving a shift toward more strategic resource allocation, enhanced operational efficiency, and ultimately, a greater impact. As nonprofits embrace AI, they will unlock new potentials in resource development, transforming challenges into opportunities for growth and innovation. This dynamic integration of AI not only can support the current needs of nonprofit organizations but also pave the way for a future where their missions are achieved more effectively and sustainably.

Capacity Factor

Imagine a small nonprofit focused on environmental conservation, operating with a lean team and limited resources. Traditionally, this "capacity factor" would have put them at a disadvantage in securing grants and funding, as larger organizations with more staff and better infrastructure tend to be favored. However, the introduction of AI into their operations can mark a turning point. Utilizing AI tools, this small organization can now efficiently analyze vast data sets to identify potential donors, tailor fundraising campaigns to match donor preferences, and automate the grant writing process to uncover and apply for relevant funding opportunities with precision.

This scenario exemplifies how AI can level the playing field in the nonprofit sector, allowing organizations of any size to enhance their capacity for resource development. The capacity factor, while still relevant, is increasingly being mitigated by AI's ability to optimize operations and extend an organization's reach and impact. Smaller nonprofits, once limited by their size, can now leverage AI to improve their planning, implementation, and sustainability of projects, making them more competitive in the quest for resources.

AI's impact extends beyond just bridging the capacity gap. It can revolutionize key functions such as fund development, grant writing, and program promotion, bringing a new era of precision and personalization to nonprofit operations. AI can enable nonprofits to develop more targeted fundraising strategies, predict donation patterns with greater accuracy, and enhance donor engagement through the use of virtual assistants and chatbots. In grant writing, AI can assist in creating more compelling proposals, identifying suitable funding opportunities, and utilizing historical data to optimize applications.

The advent of AI is transforming the nonprofit landscape, ensuring that success in resource development is not solely determined by an organization's size. By integrating AI, all nonprofits, regardless of their scale, can compete more effectively for resources, contributing significantly to their communities. This shift signifies a new paradigm in the nonprofit sector, where the capacity factor becomes one of many considerations, rather than the defining barrier to success in securing funding and implementing impactful projects. AI, therefore, is not just a technological tool but a strategic asset that empowers nonprofits to overcome traditional limitations and achieve their missions more effectively.

Grant Readiness

Grants are often the lifeline for many nonprofit organizations, serving as a crucial source of funding pivotal for their operations and initiatives. However, the journey to securing these grants transcends merely presenting a flawless project proposal. The essence of being *grant ready* takes center stage, highlighting a comprehensive readiness that encompasses more than just innovative project ideas or eloquent proposals. Grant readiness is about an organization's holistic preparation to successfully acquire and manage grant funds, underpinned significantly by the integration of AI.

AI technology can reshape how nonprofits demonstrate grant readiness, enhancing their financial management, governance structures, operational efficiency, and historical success with an unprecedented level of sophistication. AI enables detailed financial analysis and predictive budgeting, ensuring transparency and accountability that grantors seek. It streamlines governance by automating compliance tracking and policy updates, thus bolstering the organization's credibility. On the operational front, AI optimizes processes, from automating routine tasks to deploying advanced project management tools, demonstrating an organization's capacity to effectively implement and oversee proposed projects.

Moreover, AI's role in evidencing an organization's track record through data analytics and outcome predictions illustrates a robust capability to utilize funds responsibly and achieve projected outcomes. This comprehensive AI-driven approach can ensure that nonprofits are not just prepared on paper but are genuinely equipped in practice to meet the granular demands of grantors. By leveraging AI to solidify these foundational aspects of grant readiness, nonprofits can significantly enhance their prospects of securing grant funding, ensuring that their innovative and essential project ideas receive the support they

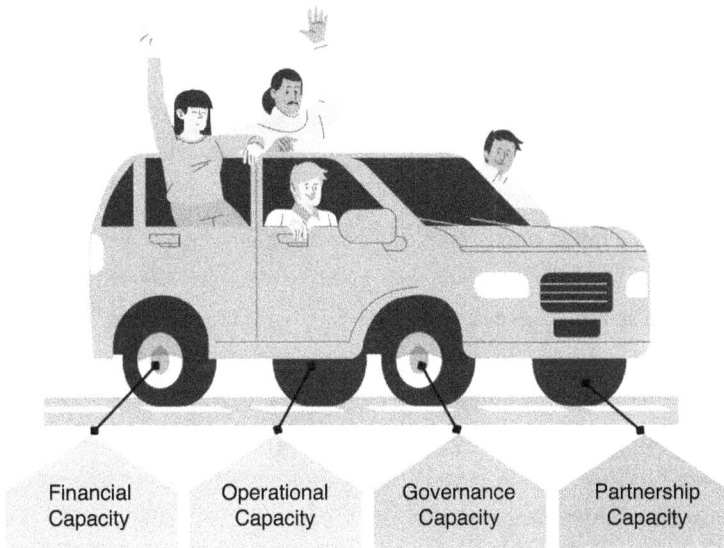

Figure 7.2 Grant readiness capacity requirements

necessitate to come to fruition. In this AI-enhanced landscape, the ability of nonprofits to secure grants is profoundly amplified, ensuring that their crucial missions receive the backing needed for successful implementation and impactful results.

In the nonprofit sector, AI is becoming an indispensable tool in enhancing grant readiness, much like a mechanic equipped with the latest technology to ensure that all four tires of a car are in prime condition, see Figure 7.2. This analogy extends to the way AI fortifies the foundational capacities crucial for grant success: financial, governance, operational, and partnership.

Imagine a nonprofit dedicated to environmental conservation, facing the common challenge of securing sufficient funding for its ambitious projects. This organization decides to leverage AI to enhance its financial capacity, transforming its approach to fund management and grant acquisition. By integrating AI into their financial systems, they automate and optimize their budgeting processes, gain predictive insights into funding trends, and identify new, untapped sources of financial support.

Financial Capacity

For example, the nonprofit uses AI algorithms to analyze historical donation data, revealing patterns that guide the development of more targeted and effective fundraising campaigns. This AI-driven approach not only boosts their donation inflow but also demonstrates to potential grantors a sophisticated level of financial management and planning capability. The organization's ability to strategically manage its resources, forecast financial needs, and adapt to funding changes becomes a testament to its grant readiness, greatly enhancing its appeal to funders.

Furthermore, by employing AI for grant writing, the nonprofit can sift through thousands of grant opportunities to find those best aligned with their mission and current projects. AI tools help them craft compelling grant proposals by analyzing successful applications from the past and suggesting improvements, increasing their success rate in securing grants.

This proactive use of AI to bolster financial capacity exemplifies how nonprofits can transform their approach to funding and grant management. Just as the AI-enhanced financial management practices provide a solid foundation for the environmental nonprofit, similar strategies can be applied across the sector. Nonprofits that adopt AI can not only streamline their operations and improve financial health but also position themselves as more capable and reliable partners to funders. This shift in financial management, powered by AI, would mark a significant step toward overcoming the traditional hurdles in grant acquisition, enabling nonprofits to secure the funds they need to achieve their missions more effectively.

AI offers nonprofit organizations a transformative capability to build financial capacity by identifying and efficiently utilizing diverse funding channels. By deploying AI-driven analytics, nonprofits can sift through extensive data sets to pinpoint funding opportunities that align with their mission and operational focus, ranging from grants and donations to innovative financing options like social impact bonds. AI algorithms analyze past funding successes and market trends to recommend the most promising channels, ensuring that efforts are concentrated where the potential for financial support is highest. Moreover, AI can optimize fundraising strategies by predicting donor behaviors, enabling personalized engagement that increases the likelihood of contributions.

For instance, AI can identify patterns in donor preferences and giving history, allowing nonprofits to tailor their communications and appeals to match donor interests closely. This strategic use of AI not only maximizes the efficiency of fundraising efforts but also significantly enhances the organization's ability to secure a stable and diversified financial base. Through the intelligent analysis and application of data, AI empowers nonprofits to navigate the complex funding landscape with greater agility and precision, building a robust financial capacity that supports sustainable growth and impact.

Operational Capacity

Integrating AI into the operational capacity of nonprofit organizations can dramatically transform their efficiency and effectiveness, acting as a pivotal force that not only enables them to act on their mission but also to showcase their impact dynamically. AI can become a catalyst in both the *act* and *show* components of operational capacity, enhancing program management, optimizing processes, and improving communication strategies.

For the *act* component, AI can streamline on-the-ground operations, making it possible for organizations to deliver their programs and services more efficiently. AI-driven project management tools can forecast potential hurdles and offer solutions in real-time, ensuring projects stay on track. Furthermore, AI can automate routine administrative tasks, allowing staff to focus on strategic activities and direct service delivery. This automation extends to volunteer management, where AI platforms match volunteers with tasks that suit their skills and interests, optimizing human resource allocation.

On the *show* side, AI can revolutionize how nonprofits communicate their impact. Through data analytics, AI evaluates the effectiveness of different communication channels and strategies, guiding organizations on where and how to share their achievements for maximum visibility. AI tools can automate the generation of reports and impact assessments, providing stakeholders with compelling evidence of the nonprofit's work and its outcomes. Social media algorithms powered by AI optimize content delivery, ensuring that messages reach broader audiences and engage community members effectively.

Moreover, AI's role in data analysis transcends operational efficiency; it enables nonprofits to glean insights from program data, feedback, and interactions, informing strategy adjustments and program improvements. This continuous learning cycle, powered by AI, ensures that nonprofits not only perform their work effectively but also remain adaptive and responsive to the needs of the communities they serve.

In balancing the *act* and *show* components, AI can provide a strategic advantage, ensuring that nonprofits do not just work behind the scenes but also gain the recognition and support necessary for their sustainability. By harnessing AI, nonprofits can elevate their operational capacity, achieving a harmonious balance between executing impactful programs and showcasing their successes. This integration of AI into operational processes can mark a significant evolution in the nonprofit sector, enabling organizations to deliver on their missions more effectively and communicate their impact more powerfully.

Governance Capacity

Governance capacity, symbolized as the third tire in this analogy, is essential for the integrity and effectiveness of a nonprofit organization. This capacity hinges on having a board that is not only effective but also deeply engaged in the organization's mission. A robust governance structure, comprising clear policies and procedures, is paramount. Such a structure ensures adherence to legal standards and ethical practices— aspects that are critically examined by grantors, diversity, equity, and inclusion (DEI) policies particularly in regions like the United States and Canada.

AI can significantly bolster the governance capacity of nonprofit organizations, acting as a sophisticated tool that refines and enhances governance structures and practices. As the third tire in our analogy, ensuring governance integrity and effectiveness is crucial, and AI can provide an innovative approach to achieving this goal.

AI revolutionizes governance by facilitating the development and maintenance of a diverse and effective board. It does so through advanced analytics and machine learning algorithms that can analyze demographic, experiential, and skill-based data to recommend board compositions that reflect a broad spectrum of perspectives and expertise. This capability is particularly valuable in promoting DEI policies, ensuring that the organization's governance body mirrors the inclusivity and variety of the community it serves.

Furthermore, AI enhances accountability within nonprofit governance. Automated systems can monitor compliance with legal and ethical standards, track decision-making processes, and ensure that responsibilities are clearly defined and adhered to. AI-driven platforms can also facilitate transparent and efficient communication with stakeholders, providing regular, detailed updates on organizational activities, achievements, and governance practices.

In terms of institutionalization, AI contributes by embedding governance policies into the organization's daily operations and culture. Through the use of AI, policies and procedures are not only established but are actively monitored and updated in response to changing regulations and organizational needs. This ensures that governance practices are not static but evolve, maintaining relevance and efficacy over time.

AI can also play a pivotal role in driving organizational excellence. Through data analysis and predictive modeling, AI tools can aid strategic planning, program evaluation, and the continuous improvement of governance practices. By providing insights into potential risks, opportunities, and performance metrics, AI empowers boards to make informed decisions that align with the organization's mission and long-term goals.

By integrating AI into governance processes, nonprofits can ensure that their governance capacity is not only compliant and effective but also dynamic and responsive to the needs of their mission and the communities they serve. AI's contribution to governance in the nonprofit sector marks a transformative shift toward more informed, efficient, and inclusive governance practices, enhancing the organization's ability to secure grants and achieve sustained impact. This adoption of AI in governance exemplifies a forward-thinking approach, positioning nonprofits for success in an increasingly complex and digital world.

Partnership Capacity

Partnership capacity, symbolized as the crucial fourth tire in this analogy, underscores the nonprofit organization's ability to establish and nurture strategic partnerships. These collaborations and networks are not merely beneficial but often pivotal in amplifying the impact of grant-funded projects and showcasing the organization's capability and reach to grantors.

AI can dramatically transform the partnership capacity of nonprofit organizations, making the task of forging and nurturing strategic partnerships more efficient and impactful. This capacity, likened to the crucial fourth tire in our analogy, is vital for amplifying the impact of initiatives and enhancing the organization's appeal to grantors through demonstrated collaborative strength.

AI revolutionizes how nonprofits identify and engage potential partners. For instance, AI-powered platforms can analyze vast data sets to identify organizations with aligned missions and complementary resources, facilitating strategic alliances. This process is akin to a sophisticated matchmaking system, where AI algorithms consider factors such as mission alignment, resource complementarity, and geographic proximity to suggest potential partnerships that could amplify impact and operational scope.

Moreover, AI enhances the initial outreach and communication with potential partners. Automated AI-driven tools can initiate contact, share organizational objectives, and explore mutual interests with a level of efficiency and scale not possible through manual efforts alone. This initial AI-facilitated dialogue paves the way for more meaningful human-to-human conversations, setting the foundation for strong collaborative relationships.

Once partnerships are established, AI continues to play a pivotal role in managing and sustaining these relationships. Collaborative project management tools, powered by AI, can streamline coordination, monitor progress, and ensure that all parties are aligned and working toward shared goals. These tools can also provide real-time updates and insights, making it easier for all involved to adapt to changes and address challenges proactively.

In the realm of showcasing collaborative impact, AI offers advanced data analytics and reporting capabilities. It can aggregate and analyze outcomes from partnership initiatives, providing clear, data-driven narratives of the collective impact. This evidence is invaluable in demonstrating the effectiveness of collaborations to existing and potential funders, reinforcing the organization's credibility and capacity to deliver on its mission through strategic alliances.

By integrating AI into the development and management of partnerships, nonprofits not only streamline operational aspects of collaborations but also deepen the strategic value of these relationships. AI empowers organizations to build a network of partnerships that are based on mutual goals, complementary strengths, and shared success, ensuring that the collective effort is greater than the sum of its parts.

The analogy of floating ants, overcoming obstacles through unity and cooperation, beautifully illustrates the essence of effective partnerships. Similarly, nonprofits, equipped with AI, can navigate challenges more successfully and achieve goals that seem unattainable when facing them alone. AI's role in enhancing partnership capacity is a testament to the power of collaboration in the nonprofit sector, enabling organizations to extend their reach, amplify their impact, and achieve greater success in their missions.

CHAPTER 8

Financial Management

Beware of little expenses; a small leak will sink a great ship.[1]

—**Benjamin Franklin**

Reflecting on my time on the board of a small to medium-sized charity, I vividly recall the challenges we faced with financial forecasting and strategic planning. One of the most daunting periods was when we grappled with the uncertainty of what would happen in the upcoming three months as our existing grants were coming to an end.

I remember the discussions we had, filled with a sense of apprehension. We were in a position where we didn't have a clear understanding of our fixed and operational costs. This lack of clarity made it incredibly difficult to plan effectively for the future. The questions of financial sustainability were always at the forefront, yet the answers were elusive.

The most challenging part, for me, was the discussion about our team—who we might have to let go and who we could retain under various financial scenarios. These were not just theoretical exercises in budgeting; they were decisions that would impact real people's lives, people who had dedicated themselves to our mission.

This experience highlighted for me the crucial importance of having robust financial management systems in place. It became clear that without comprehensive financial data and effective tools for analysis, making informed strategic decisions was nearly impossible.

I realized the value of predictive tools like AI in such scenarios. AI's ability to analyze past financial trends, monitor current expenditures, and even predict future financial conditions could have provided us with much-needed insights. These insights are not just about numbers— they are about guiding an organization through uncertain times with informed confidence, ensuring that every decision aligns with both immediate needs and long-term sustainability.

Looking back, I see this period as a learning curve, one that underscored the complexities of financial planning in the nonprofit sector and the indispensable need for advanced tools and strategies to navigate such challenges effectively.

In the nonprofit sector, leaders often face the challenge of comprehending the complex financial landscape that these organizations operate within. This difficulty largely stems from the diversified funding structure common in nonprofits, as well as the intricate web of projects financed by different funders, each with their own specific timelines and reporting requirements.

The diversity of funding sources—ranging from grants, donations, and fundraising events to government contracts and sometimes service fees—contributes to a multifaceted financial environment. Each funding stream may come with its unique restrictions, conditions, and reporting standards. For instance, a grant from a foundation might be earmarked specifically for a particular program with strict guidelines on how the funds are to be used and reported, while donations received from individual supporters could have fewer restrictions.

Managing these diverse funding streams effectively requires a nuanced understanding of each source's particularities. This can be a daunting task for leaders, especially those who may not have a background in finance or nonprofit management. Additionally, the projects funded by these various sources may run on different schedules and timelines, adding another layer of complexity to financial oversight.

Furthermore, financial reporting in nonprofits is not just about accounting for funds but also about demonstrating the impact of those funds. Different funders often require different formats of reporting and distinct metrics of success, making the process of financial reporting multifaceted and time-consuming.

This complex financial landscape can make it challenging for leaders to have a clear and comprehensive understanding of the organization's financial health and accountability. It underscores the need for effective financial management systems within nonprofits and the importance of financial literacy and training for its leaders. Ensuring that they are equipped with the knowledge and tools to understand and oversee the organization's finances is crucial for effective governance and the long-term sustainability of the nonprofit.

Every Penny Counts

In the chapter dedicated to financial management, one cannot overlook the timeless wisdom encapsulated in Benjamin Franklin's quote: "Beware of little expenses; a small leak will sink a great ship." This adage is particularly pertinent in the context of nonprofit financial management, where every dollar counts, and the efficient allocation of resources is crucial.

Franklin's words serve as a powerful reminder of the importance of vigilance in managing even the smallest expenses. In the nonprofit sector, operating often with limited budgets and reliant on funding that can be sporadic, the impact of seemingly minor expenditures can accumulate over time, leading to significant financial strain. This analogy of a small leak sinking a great ship aptly illustrates how small, unchecked expenses can cumulatively create a substantial drain on an organization's financial health.

For nonprofits, this means that careful budgeting and close monitoring of expenditures are not just good practices but essential ones. It involves scrutinizing every expense, no matter how small, and assessing its necessity and alignment with the organization's goals and mission. This approach to financial management is about being proactive rather than reactive—preventing the *small leaks* before they become significant problems.

Implementing regular financial reviews, setting strict budgetary guidelines, and fostering a culture of financial responsibility across the organization are critical steps in this direction. It's also about under-standing that cost cutting doesn't always mean cutting corners. Instead, it's about making smart choices that maximize impact while minimizing unnecessary expenditures.

Furthermore, this principle extends to seeking ways to enhance efficiency. Leveraging technology, negotiating better rates with vendors, and finding innovative ways to reduce costs are all part of a strategic approach to financial management that pays heed to Franklin's advice.

The essence of effective financial management in the nonprofit sector can often be found in the attention paid to the small details. By being mindful of *little expenses* and understanding their potential cumulative impact, nonprofits can safeguard their financial stability, ensuring that they remain capable and ready to fulfill their mission without being capsized by financial challenges.

How Can AI Help

AI can bring several benefits to the nonprofit sector in relation to financial management, enhancing efficiency, accuracy, and strategic decision making.

For bigger organizations, AI-driven analytics can provide valuable decision support for financial planning and strategy. By analyzing financial data and market trends, AI can assist them in making informed decisions about investments, cost-saving measures, and long-term financial planning.

AI-powered predictive analytics can also assist those nonprofits in creating more accurate and dynamic budgets. By analyzing historical financial data, economic indicators, and other relevant factors, AI can predict future trends and help organizations make informed decisions about budget allocation. This enables nonprofits to optimize their financial resources and respond effectively to changing circumstances.

AI tools can also automate compliance monitoring processes, ensuring that nonprofits adhere to financial regulations and reporting requirements. By flagging potential compliance issues, these tools help organizations stay in compliance with legal and regulatory standards, reducing the risk of penalties and reputational damage.

For smaller nonprofits organizations, AI can be particularly beneficial given their limited staffing capacity.

AI-powered tools can automate data entry processes and streamline bookkeeping tasks. By employing machine learning algorithms, these systems can categorize transactions, reconcile accounts, and maintain accurate financial records. For smaller organizations with no dedicated bookkeeper, this not only reduces the risk of errors but also frees up valuable time for focusing on service delivery.

AI can enhance expense tracking by automatically categorizing and analyzing transactions. Additionally, machine learning algorithms can detect unusual patterns or anomalies in financial data, aiding in the early identification of potential fraud. This proactive approach to fraud detection helps safeguard the integrity of financial transactions and ensures that funds are used appropriately.

By predicting revenue and expense patterns AI can assist nonprofits in optimizing cash flow. This is particularly valuable for smaller nonprofits with fluctuating income streams and diverse funding sources.

Incorporating AI into financial management processes empowers nonprofits to operate more efficiently, make data-driven decisions, and allocate resources strategically, ultimately enhancing their ability to fulfill their missions and make a positive impact on the communities they serve.

Bookkeeping

AI has the potential to greatly assist in the financial management of nonprofit organizations in several ways, one of the most notable being automated data entry and financial bookkeeping. This application of AI technology is revolutionizing these traditionally time-consuming and error-prone tasks, turning them into streamlined and efficient processes. By harnessing AI for these critical functions, nonprofits can significantly enhance their financial management capabilities.

Automated data entry through AI brings a new level of accuracy and speed to managing financial records. Traditionally, bookkeeping in nonprofits involves manually inputting data from various sources— donations, grants, expenses, and more—into accounting systems. This not only consumes valuable time but also poses the risk of human error, which can lead to financial discrepancies. AI-powered tools, however, can process this data with remarkable precision and at a fraction of the time it would take a human. They are capable of extracting information from various documents and digital platforms, ensuring that all entries are accurate and up-to-date.

Furthermore, AI in bookkeeping extends beyond mere data entry. It encompasses the categorization and reconciliation of financial transactions, streamlining the entire accounting cycle. For example, an AI system can categorize expenses and income into appropriate accounts based on its learning from past entries, facilitating a more organized and accessible financial record. This capability is particularly beneficial for nonprofits, where funds often need to be allocated and reported in specific categories as per donor or grant requirements.

The automation of these processes significantly reduces the workload on nonprofit staff, allowing them to focus more on strategic tasks rather than getting bogged down with administrative duties. It also minimizes the risk of errors in financial reporting, which is crucial for maintaining the trust of donors and stakeholders. Timely and accurate financial reports are essential for decision making, budgeting, and demonstrating accountability and transparency—all critical aspects of successful nonprofit management.

Moreover, AI-driven bookkeeping supports better financial analysis. With data accurately captured and organized, nonprofits can use AI tools to gain insights into financial trends, cash flow patterns, and areas where cost-efficiency can be improved. This analytical aspect of AI empowers nonprofits to make more informed decisions, optimize their resources, and plan more effectively for the future.

The use of AI for automated data entry and bookkeeping marks a significant step forward in the financial management of nonprofit organizations. By embracing these AI-powered tools, nonprofits can achieve higher accuracy, efficiency, and insight in their financial operations, paving the way for greater organizational effectiveness and impact.

Managerial Accounting Versus Financial Accounting

It's crucial to understand the distinct roles and purposes of financial accounting and managerial accounting. While both are essential for the effective financial management of a nonprofit, they serve different needs and audiences.

While financial accounting and managerial accounting both deal with the financial aspects of a nonprofit, they serve different but complementary purposes. Financial accounting is about accuracy and compliance, providing a clear, standardized view of the organization's finances to those outside the organization. Managerial accounting, meanwhile, is a tool for internal decision making, offering detailed and flexible reports and analyses to help manage the organization effectively. Both are crucial for the sound financial management of a nonprofit, ensuring not only compliance and transparency but also strategic effectiveness and sustainability.

Financial Accounting: The External Perspective

Financial accounting is primarily concerned with the preparation of financial statements—the balance sheet, income statement, and cash flow statement. Its primary purpose is to provide an accurate and standardized view of the organization's financial position to external stakeholders. These stakeholders include donors, grantors, regulatory bodies, and the general public.

Financial accounting is governed by strict rules and standards, such as Generally Accepted Accounting Principles (GAAP) in the United States or Canada Revenue Agency regulations in Canada. The focus is on historical data and adherence to accounting norms to ensure consistency and comparability. Financial accounting provides a snapshot of the organization's financial health and activities over a specific period. It's about transparency and accountability, ensuring that the nonprofit is responsibly managing the funds it receives.

AI can significantly assist financial accounting in various ways, enhancing efficiency, accuracy, and overall effectiveness. In the specific context of financial accounting, AI's capabilities can be leveraged to transform traditional accounting practices:

- Automating routine tasks: AI excels at automating repetitive and time-consuming tasks such as data entry, categorization of expenses and revenues, and reconciliation of accounts. This automation reduces the time accountants spend on routine tasks, allowing them to focus on more complex and strategic activities.
- Enhancing accuracy: AI algorithms are adept at processing large volumes of financial data with high precision, reducing the likelihood of human error. This increased accuracy is crucial in financial accounting, where even small errors can have significant implications.
- Improving compliance and reporting: AI can keep track of the latest regulatory and compliance requirements, ensuring that financial statements and reports adhere to current standards such as Generally Accepted Accounting Principles (GAAP) or International Financial Reporting Standards (IFRS). It can automatically update reporting templates and flag any potential compliance issues.

- Enhancing audit processes: AI can improve the efficiency and effectiveness of audit processes by analyzing entire datasets rather than just samples. This comprehensive analysis can provide a more accurate and complete view of financial transactions and records.

Managerial Accounting: The Internal Tool

Managerial accounting, on the other hand, is more internally focused. It's about providing detailed financial and operational information to the organization's management to aid in decision making. Unlike financial accounting, which is retrospective and standardized, managerial accounting is often forward-looking and flexible. It can be tailored to meet the specific needs of the organization.

This form of accounting includes budgeting, forecasting, cost analysis, and evaluation of financial performance against strategic goals. Managerial accounting helps nonprofit leaders make informed decisions about resource allocation, program effectiveness, and strategic planning. It provides insights into how funds can be optimally utilized to further the mission of the organization.

AI can greatly enhance managerial accounting, a branch of accounting focused on providing internal management with the information necessary to make informed business decisions. AI's integration into managerial accounting can revolutionize how nonprofits approach and utilize their financial data for strategic planning and operational efficiency.

- Budgeting and forecasting: AI can analyze historical financial data and current market trends to create more accurate and dynamic budget forecasts. By predicting future financial scenarios, AI aids managerial accountants in planning budgets that are both realistic and adaptable to changing conditions.
- Cost analysis and reduction: AI can identify patterns and anomalies in spending, helping organizations understand where they can cut costs without compromising the quality of their

services. This analysis can be vital for nonprofits operating on tight budgets, ensuring efficient use of resources.

- Performance measurement: AI tools can track and analyze key performance indicators related to financial health, such as cash flow, profit margins, and revenue growth. This provides management with a clear view of the organization's financial performance and helps in making informed strategic decisions.

- Customized reporting: AI systems can generate detailed financial reports tailored to the specific needs of different managers or departments within the organization. These customized reports provide relevant insights for various roles, enhancing decision making at all levels of the organization.

- Real-time decision-making support: With AI, managerial accountants can access real-time financial data and analytics, allowing for quick and informed decision making in response to emerging opportunities or challenges.

- Real-time financial analysis and reporting: AI enables real-time processing and analysis of financial data, offering up-to-date insights into an organization's financial health. This immediacy can be particularly beneficial for timely decision making and reporting.

- Predictive analytics: AI can analyze historical financial data to identify trends and make predictions about future financial scenarios. This capability aids in forecasting revenues, expenses, and cash flow, which is essential for strategic planning and financial management.

- Fraud detection: AI systems can monitor financial transactions to detect anomalies or patterns indicative of fraudulent activity. Early detection is key to minimizing financial losses and maintaining the integrity of financial records.

- Predictive analytics for operational efficiency: AI can forecast future trends in operational costs and revenues, enabling nonprofits to optimize their operations proactively. This foresight can be crucial in resource allocation and long-term strategic planning.

- Enhancing risk management: AI can identify potential financial risks by analyzing various internal and external factors. This proactive approach to risk management allows nonprofits to strategize effectively to mitigate potential financial setbacks.

In integrating AI into managerial accounting, nonprofits can gain a deeper and more nuanced understanding of their financial operations. This leads to more strategic resource management, better alignment of financial strategies with organizational goals, and overall improved operational efficiency. AI's predictive and analytical capabilities make it an invaluable tool for managerial accountants, driving data-driven decision making and strategic planning.

Predictive Analytics for Budgeting

AI's ability to access and analyze data on economic developments at local, regional, and global levels empowers nonprofit organizations to make more accurate and informed projections about their financial future.

Traditionally, financial forecasting has been based on historical data and manual analysis, often limited by the scope of human capacity and the availability of current information. However, AI transforms this process by leveraging vast amounts of data, encompassing not just an organization's internal financial history but also external economic indicators. This includes trends in the global economy, regional market fluctuations, and local financial developments, all of which can have profound impacts on a nonprofit's financial health.

By integrating these diverse data sources, AI can provide a more comprehensive view of potential financial futures. Its advanced algorithms can detect patterns and correlations that might be invisible to human analysts. This enables AI to make predictions about future financial conditions, such as changes in donor behavior, fluctuations in grant availability, shifts in economic conditions that affect fundraising efforts, and more.

For nonprofit leaders, this level of insight is invaluable. It allows them to be better prepared for future challenges and opportunities.

With AI-driven financial forecasting, they can anticipate potential financial downturns and plan accordingly, ensuring the organization remains resilient and sustainable. Conversely, AI can also highlight potential areas of growth and investment, helping boards to strategically allocate resources where they will have the most significant impact.

Furthermore, AI's predictive power enhances leaders' ability to engage in proactive rather than reactive decision making. Instead of merely responding to financial changes as they occur, boards can implement strategies based on predictive insights, positioning their organizations to thrive in an ever-changing financial landscape.

In summary, AI's role in financial forecasting for nonprofits is not just about making predictions; it's about providing a strategic tool that helps its leaders navigate the complexities of financial planning in a dynamic world. By harnessing the power of AI, nonprofit leaders can ensure that their organizations are not only prepared for the future but are also equipped to make the most of it.

CHAPTER 9

Program Development and Project Management

The biggest challenge in project management is to ensure that you are not just managing projects but leading them.[1]

—**Amit Kalantri**

Let's chat about something that's pretty common in the nonprofit world —the way grants work. Did you know that the majority of grants in the nonprofit sector are usually earmarked for new projects? Yeah, it's a thing! These funds are typically directed toward kickstarting new initiatives rather than covering administrative costs or routine operations.

This focus on projects means that most nonprofits, especially medium-sized ones, are often juggling multiple projects at any given time. Imagine having over 10 different projects, each with its own set of goals, timelines, and challenges, running simultaneously. That's the reality for many nonprofit organizations! It's like having several different pots on the stove, each needing its own ingredients and cooking time, and all of them needing to be watched carefully.

So, how do nonprofits handle this? Well, it's all about balance and organization. Each project is like a unique puzzle piece that fits into the larger picture of the organization's mission. Project managers in nonprofits become experts at multitasking and prioritizing. They have to keep track of various deadlines, budgets, and team dynamics, making sure that every project is moving forward as planned.

This is where strong project management comes into play. It's crucial to have a clear understanding of each project's objectives and how they contribute to the overall goals of the nonprofit. Effective communication is key. Everyone involved, from team members to stakeholders, needs to be on the same page. Regular meetings, updates, and check-ins become part of the daily routine.

Of course, managing multiple projects is no walk in the park. There are always challenges like resource allocation, unforeseen obstacles, and sometimes, shifting priorities. But it's also an opportunity for growth and innovation. Every new project is a chance to make a difference, to learn something new, and to build stronger, more effective teams.

In the nonprofit sector, where projects are the heart of the workflow, being adept at managing multiple projects is not just an asset; it's a necessity. It's about more than just keeping the balls in the air; it's about ensuring that each one is adding value to the organization and, ultimately, to the community it serves.

Amit Kalantri's insightful quote, "The biggest challenge in project management is to ensure that you are not just managing projects but leading them," speaks volumes about the nuanced difference between mere management and leadership within the context of project management. This statement underscores the idea that managing a project isn't solely about ticking boxes, meeting deadlines, and staying within budget. While these aspects are undoubtedly important, true project leadership goes beyond these fundamentals. It involves inspiring and guiding the team toward a shared vision, fostering a collaborative environment, and navigating through challenges with strategic insight and adaptability.

A project manager, in the role of a leader, not only oversees the logistical aspects of a project but also motivates the team, harnessing their skills and channeling their efforts toward innovative solutions and excellence. This approach transforms a project from a routine task into a journey of collective growth and achievement, where the journey's value is as significant as the destination. Thus, the essence of this quote lies in recognizing and embracing the broader, more dynamic role of a project manager as a leader who drives progress, cultivates a positive team culture, and steers the project to success with vision and foresight.

Diving into the concept of program management in the nonprofit sector offers a glimpse into a realm where coordination, synergy, and strategic oversight come together beautifully. Picture a tapestry where each thread represents an individual project. When these threads intertwine, they create a more impactful and cohesive design. This is the essence of program management—a process that involves overseeing a collection of related projects or ones that overlap in goals or beneficiaries.

In the nonprofit world, program management is akin to conducting an orchestra. Each musician (project) plays their part, contributing to a harmonious and unified whole. The role of the program manager is to ensure that while each project achieves its individual objectives, it also aligns and contributes to the broader, strategic goals of the program.

This approach offers numerous benefits, including enhanced impact, more efficient resource utilization, and improved collaboration across projects. While managing a program comes with its challenges—like juggling different timelines, budgets, and team dynamics—the rewards of creating a sum greater than its parts make it a crucial aspect of nonprofit management. Program management, in essence, weaves individual projects into a cohesive program, maximizing their collective impact on the community they serve.

In simple terms, program management is about overseeing a collection of related projects, or sometimes projects that have overlaps in goals or beneficiaries. It's like being a conductor of an orchestra where each musician (or project) plays a different instrument, but all contribute to a harmonious and unified piece of music.

The idea behind managing these projects collectively as a program is pretty straightforward yet powerful. It's all about synergy. By managing related projects under one umbrella, nonprofits can ensure that these projects are not just achieving their individual objectives but are also working together seamlessly toward a broader, strategic goal.

Think of a program manager in a nonprofit as someone who has a bird's eye view of multiple projects. They need to understand how these projects interlink, where they can support each other, and where they need to tread carefully to avoid overlaps or conflicts. It's a balancing act of sorts—making sure that while each project thrives in its own right, it also contributes positively to the larger program goals.

Managing a program comes with its unique set of challenges. The program manager needs to be adept at juggling different project timelines, budgets, and team dynamics. They also need to be great communicators, as they're the link between individual project teams and the broader organizational strategy.

But the rewards? They're significant. Effective program management can lead to greater impact, more efficient use of resources, and enhanced collaboration across projects. It's about creating a sum that's greater than its parts.

So, in essence, program management in the nonprofit world is about weaving individual projects into a cohesive and impactful program. It's about ensuring that all these projects, while distinct in their objectives and

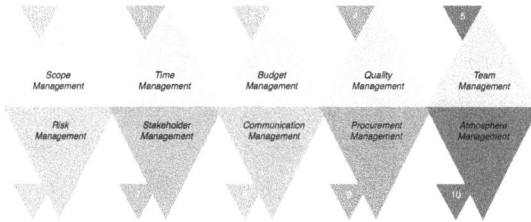

Figure 9.1 Project management components

execution, come together to create a bigger, more meaningful impact on the community they serve.

Project Management Areas

Project management is a multifaceted discipline, crucial for the successful execution of projects in any organization. It encompasses several key components as illustrated in Figure 9.1, each playing a vital role in ensuring the project meets its objectives efficiently and effectively.

Each of these components plays a crucial role in the overall success of a project. By effectively managing these aspects, project managers can ensure that their projects are not only completed on time and within budget but also meet the desired quality standards and achieve the intended outcomes.

Time Management

This involves the strategic planning, scheduling, and tracking of project timelines and activities. Effective time management ensures that the project progresses on schedule and meets its deadlines.

In the nonprofit sector, where resources are often limited and the impact is crucial, effective time management in project management can be a game-changer. Nonprofits typically juggle multiple projects, each with its own set of deadlines and objectives, making efficient time management a critical skill. Here, AI can play a transformative role, and real-life examples illustrate how AI contributes to this crucial aspect.

For instance, consider a nonprofit organization focused on environmental conservation. They may have various initiatives, like community clean-up drives, educational workshops, and policy advocacy campaigns, running concurrently. AI can assist in strategically planning these initiatives. By analyzing past project data, AI can predict how long different types of projects are likely to take, helping the organization to create more realistic schedules.

AI tools can also automatically schedule tasks and allocate resources based on the availability of staff and volunteers. This automation significantly reduces the manual effort involved in planning and allows project managers to focus on higher-value activities like stakeholder engagement and impact assessment.

A real-life example of this is seen in nonprofit organizations that organize fundraising events. An AI-driven project management tool can optimize the event planning process by suggesting the best dates for the event based on past attendance data, avoiding clashes with other community events, and even predicting the best times for certain activities during the event.

Another area where AI contributes significantly is in tracking and monitoring the progress of projects. Nonprofits can use AI tools to automatically track the progress of their initiatives against their timelines. For example, an AI system can send alerts if a project is falling behind schedule or if there are discrepancies in the allocated resources. This allows for quick adjustments, ensuring that projects stay on track.

A compelling case study is in the context of disaster relief operations. Here, time management is not just important; it's critical. AI can assist in quickly analyzing the situation, prioritizing tasks, and efficiently deploying resources. For example, an AI system can analyze data from various sources to identify the most affected areas and prioritize relief efforts accordingly. This ensures that help reaches where it's needed most, and quickly.

In the nonprofit sector, where the stakes are high and resources are often stretched, AI's contribution to effective time management can have a significant impact. By aiding in strategic planning, optimizing schedules, and ensuring timely project execution, AI can help nonprofits achieve their mission-critical goals more efficiently and effectively.

Budget Management

Budget management plays a critical role in ensuring the success and sustainability of projects. Effective budget management involves accurately estimating costs, wisely allocating resources, and meticulously controlling expenditures to ensure that projects are completed within their financial constraints. This is particularly vital in the nonprofit world, where funds are often derived from donations, grants, or limited public funding, making the efficient use of every dollar crucial.

Incorporating AI into budget management transforms this crucial aspect of project management, especially in the nonprofit sector where every financial resource counts toward making a meaningful impact. AI can profoundly enhance the efficiency and effectiveness of budget management processes, from estimation to allocation and expenditure control.

AI's role in budget estimation is pivotal. By leveraging historical data and predictive analytics, AI can provide more accurate and data-driven cost estimations, considering various factors that might affect the project's financial needs. This precision in forecasting helps nonprofits prepare more realistic budgets, reducing the risk of unexpected financial shortfalls.

When it comes to resource allocation, AI can offer valuable insights to ensure funds are distributed optimally across different project components. AI algorithms can analyze past project outcomes relative to budget allocations to identify spending patterns that maximize impact. This analysis helps nonprofits make informed decisions on where to allocate resources to achieve the best possible outcomes within their budgetary constraints.

Expenditure control is another area where AI can make a significant difference. AI systems can continuously monitor project spending, comparing actual expenditures against the budget in real time. This allows for immediate identification of budget overruns or under-utilization, enabling timely adjustments. Furthermore, AI can assist in identifying potential cost-saving opportunities without compromising project quality, such as suggesting more cost-effective materials or methods based on predictive analytics.

AI also enhances transparency and accountability in budget management. With AI-driven tools, nonprofits can generate detailed financial reports effortlessly, providing stakeholders with clear insights into how funds are being utilized and the financial health of the project. This level of transparency is crucial for maintaining trust with donors, sponsors, and other stakeholders.

Quality Management

Quality management is a pivotal component in project management, particularly within the nonprofit sector, where the impact and credibility of an organization hinges on the quality of its outputs and services. This aspect of project management is not merely about meeting certain standards; it's about fulfilling, and often exceeding, the expectations of various stakeholders, including donors, beneficiaries, and community partners.

Integrating AI into quality management offers a revolutionary approach for nonprofits to ensure their project deliverables consistently meet and exceed required standards and stakeholder expectations. AI can significantly enhance each phase of quality management—planning, assurance, and control—by providing advanced tools for analysis, monitoring, and feedback.

In the planning phase, AI can assist nonprofits in defining and setting quality standards tailored to specific project objectives. Through predictive analytics and historical data analysis, AI can provide insights into achievable quality benchmarks and help identify the most effective methodologies to attain them. For example, AI can analyze past project outcomes to suggest optimal performance indicators or quality thresholds that align with both the nonprofit's mission and stakeholder expectations.

During the quality assurance phase, AI's real-time monitoring capabilities come into play. AI systems can continually assess project processes against the established quality standards, providing immediate feedback to project managers. This allows for proactive adjustments to be made, ensuring that the project remains aligned with its quality objectives. For instance, AI can track the progress of a health outreach program, monitoring service delivery rates, and beneficiary feedback to ensure the program is meeting its intended impact goals.

In the quality control stage, AI can automate the evaluation of project outputs, comparing them against the predefined quality criteria. This not only speeds up the quality control process but also introduces a level of precision that manual evaluations might lack. If a nonprofit is distributing educational materials, AI can assess the content's effectiveness, relevance, and accessibility, ensuring it meets the established educational standards and learner needs.

Moreover, AI can facilitate a more dynamic and responsive approach to quality management. By harnessing AI's capabilities, nonprofits can adapt their quality standards and processes in real-time, based on ongoing feedback and evolving project conditions. This adaptability is crucial in the fast-changing environments where many nonprofits operate.

Quality management enables nonprofits to uphold the highest standards of excellence in their projects. By leveraging AI for planning, assurance, and control, organizations can ensure their initiatives are impactful, sustainable, and aligned with both their mission and the expectations of their stakeholders. This AI-enhanced approach not only bolsters the effectiveness of nonprofit projects but also strengthens the trust and support of donors, beneficiaries, and the wider community.

Team Management

Team management in the context of project management, especially within the nonprofit sector, is an indispensable element that goes beyond mere coordination and administration. It's about creating a cohesive unit that works toward a common goal with enthusiasm and commitment. This aspect of project management is critical because the success of any project heavily relies on the effectiveness of its team.

Integrating AI into team management can profoundly enhance the way nonprofit project teams operate, communicate, and collaborate, bringing a new dimension of efficiency and effectiveness to their endeavors. AI's role in team management isn't just about automation or data analysis; it's about fostering a more dynamic, responsive, and engaged team environment.

AI-driven tools can assist in various facets of team management, starting with task allocation and scheduling. By analyzing team members' skills, past performance, and current workload, AI can help project managers assign tasks in a way that optimizes each member's strengths and preferences, enhancing job satisfaction and productivity.

Communication and collaboration are the lifelines of effective team management, and AI can play a pivotal role here as well. AI-powered communication platforms can provide real-time translation services, breaking down language barriers in diverse teams, and sentiment analysis tools can gauge team morale, alerting leaders to potential issues before they escalate.

When it comes to motivation and engagement, AI can offer personalized insights. By analyzing individual performance data, AI can recommend tailored professional development opportunities, suggest breaks or workload adjustments when stress levels seem high, and even identify achievements that warrant recognition, helping leaders maintain high team morale.

AI also brings a new level of sophistication to monitoring and evaluating team performance. Beyond traditional metrics, AI can analyze a range of data points to provide a more nuanced view of team dynamics, productivity, and collaboration efficiency. This can inform not just performance evaluations but also strategic decisions about team structure, project planning, and resource allocation.

For remote or distributed nonprofit teams, AI-enhanced management tools can be particularly transformative. They can facilitate seamless collaboration across different time zones, streamline document sharing and project updates, and even predict and mitigate potential miscommunications or project roadblocks, ensuring that geographical distances do not impede project progress.

Integrating AI into team management within the nonprofit sector is about harnessing technology to create a more connected, engaged, and effective team. It's about leveraging AI's capabilities to enhance the human elements of teamwork—communication, collaboration, and motivation—ensuring that teams are not just efficient but also resilient, adaptable, and aligned with their mission. This AI-enhanced approach to team management represents a significant step forward in enabling nonprofits to achieve their project goals and amplify their impact.

Risk Management

Risk management is a critical component in project management, especially in the nonprofit sector where resources are often limited and the stakes high. It involves a proactive approach to identifying, analyzing, and preparing for potential risks that could impact the project. Effective risk management is key to ensuring that a project not only stays on track but also achieves its objectives with minimal disruption.

AI can profoundly augment risk management in nonprofit project management, offering advanced capabilities to foresee, evaluate, and navigate risks more effectively. By integrating AI, nonprofits can leverage predictive analytics and machine learning to transform their approach to identifying and mitigating risks, ensuring their projects are more resilient and successful.

The integration of AI begins with the enhanced identification of potential risks. AI algorithms can sift through vast datasets, identifying patterns and correlations that may elude human analysis. This capability allows nonprofits to anticipate risks based on historical data, current trends, and even predictive modeling, covering a broader spectrum of potential challenges, from funding fluctuations to operational hiccups.

Once risks are identified, AI's analytical prowess comes into play in the risk analysis and prioritization phase. AI can assess the probability and potential impact of each risk, employing sophisticated models that consider various factors and scenarios. This nuanced analysis helps nonprofits focus their resources and attention on the most pressing risks, ensuring that their risk management efforts are both strategic and efficient.

Developing a risk management plan with AI's assistance enables a more dynamic and responsive strategy. AI can suggest tailored risk mitigation or transfer strategies based on the specific context and characteristics of each risk. For instance, AI could recommend diversification of funding sources based on patterns of past funding disruptions or suggest proactive stakeholder engagement strategies in response to anticipated regulatory changes.

The implementation and monitoring phase of risk management also benefit significantly from AI. Real-time monitoring and alert systems powered by AI can track risk indicators, providing immediate notifications about potential issues and enabling rapid response to mitigate impacts. This continuous monitoring ensures that risk management strategies are always aligned with the current risk landscape, allowing for timely adjustments in response to emerging threats or changes in the project environment.

In essence, incorporating AI into risk management empowers nonprofits to not only anticipate and prepare for potential risks but also to respond with agility and informed confidence. This AI-enhanced approach ensures that nonprofits can safeguard their projects against uncertainties, maximize resource efficiency, and maintain a steady course toward achieving their mission-critical objectives.

Stakeholder Management

Stakeholder management is a fundamental aspect of project management, particularly in the nonprofit sector where success often hinges on the support and engagement of various stakeholders. This process involves identifying all individuals, groups, or organizations that may be impacted by the project, and effectively managing their expectations and needs. Proper stakeholder management is essential to ensure that the project not only achieves its goals but also fosters positive relationships and maintains the organization's reputation.

Integrating AI into stakeholder management can significantly transform how nonprofits identify, understand, and engage with their stakeholders. AI-driven tools can analyze vast amounts of data to map out stakeholder landscapes, predict stakeholder behaviors, and tailor engagement strategies, ensuring a more effective and dynamic approach to managing stakeholder relationships.

AI can streamline the identification of stakeholders by analyzing project scopes, past initiatives, and community data to pinpoint individuals and groups likely to be impacted by or interested in the project. This advanced analysis helps in creating a comprehensive stakeholder map, ensuring no key player is overlooked.

Understanding stakeholders' needs and expectations becomes more nuanced with AI. Through sentiment analysis of social media, surveys, and other communication channels, AI can provide insights into stakeholders' perceptions, concerns, and expectations. This information is crucial for developing strategies that resonate with stakeholders, addressing their needs, and aligning their expectations with the project's goals.

AI enhances engagement with stakeholders by personalizing communication. Based on stakeholders' interaction history, preferences, and feedback, AI can help tailor messages, choose the most effective communication channels, and determine optimal engagement times. This personalized approach can significantly boost stakeholder engagement and support.

Ongoing communication is vital in stakeholder management, and AI can automate regular updates and feedback loops, ensuring stakeholders are consistently informed and their input is valued. AI tools can also monitor stakeholder sentiment over time, providing real-time feedback on how stakeholder attitudes are evolving with the project's progression.

Conflict resolution is another area where AI can assist. By predicting potential conflicts based on historical data and current interactions, AI can alert managers to address issues proactively. Additionally, AI can suggest strategies or communication approaches that have successfully resolved similar conflicts in the past.

In summary, AI's role in stakeholder management is transformative, offering a more strategic, responsive, and personalized approach to engaging with the diverse groups that impact and are impacted by nonprofit projects. By harnessing the power of AI, nonprofits can ensure their projects are not only successful in achieving their goals but also in building positive, enduring relationships with their stakeholders, which is crucial for long-term success and impact.

Communication Management

Communication management is a cornerstone in project management, particularly critical in the nonprofit sector, where clear and effective communication can greatly influence a project's success. It involves meticulously planning how information related to the project is shared among all stakeholders and ensuring that this dissemination is both timely and accurate. Effective communication management is vital to keep everyone aligned, informed, and engaged throughout the project's life cycle.

The integration of AI into communication management opens new avenues for enhancing the clarity, efficiency, and impact of project communications. AI tools can automate routine communication tasks, personalize messages for different stakeholder groups, and analyze the effectiveness of various communication strategies, providing valuable insights for continuous improvement.

Developing a comprehensive communication plan is the initial step, where AI can assist in identifying the most effective communication channels and strategies for different stakeholder groups. For instance, AI-driven analytics can reveal which communication platforms are most frequented by different segments of your audience, allowing for a more targeted and impactful communication approach.

Selecting the right channels is crucial, and here, AI offers the capability to segment audiences and tailor messages to suit diverse groups. Whether it's through automated e-mails, social media posts, or virtual community meetings, AI ensures that the message is not just sent but also resonates with the audience.

Timeliness and accuracy are non-negotiable in effective communication. AI systems can monitor project developments in real-time, triggering timely updates to stakeholders, thereby maintaining a consistent and reliable flow of information. For instance, if a project encounters unforeseen delays, AI can help quickly disseminate this information, explaining the situation and mitigating any potential misunderstandings or frustrations.

Moreover, AI can elevate the engagement level of communications. By analyzing past interactions, AI can help craft messages that are not only clear and concise but also engaging and resonant with the audience's values and interests. This is particularly crucial in storytelling, where AI can help shape narratives that vividly illustrate the project's impact, drawing deeper stakeholder engagement.

Feedback loops are integral to refining communication strategies, and AI enhances this aspect by offering tools for gathering and analyzing feedback across various channels. This continuous loop of feedback and improvement helps in fine-tuning communication strategies, ensuring they remain dynamic and responsive to stakeholder needs.

Incorporating AI into communication management transforms it from a static, one-way dissemination of information into a dynamic, interactive, and responsive process. It not only streamlines communication processes but also ensures that communications are more personalized, impactful, and aligned with the project's goals and stakeholder expectations. By leveraging AI, nonprofits can elevate their communication management, fostering a more engaged, informed, and collaborative project environment.

Procurement Management

Procurement management, a critical component of project management, is particularly vital in the nonprofit sector, where the judicious use of resources is directly linked to project success and organizational credibility. This process involves strategically sourcing and acquiring the necessary goods and services, ensuring these purchases align with project objectives, budget constraints, and quality expectations.

Integrating AI into procurement management can significantly enhance this process. AI can assist in identifying procurement needs by analyzing project requirements and historical data to predict what goods and services will be necessary. This predictive analysis helps in proactive procurement planning, ensuring that projects have what they need when they need it, without last-minute scrambles or overpurchasing.

When it comes to sourcing and selecting vendors, AI can transform the process by automating the evaluation of potential suppliers. AI algorithms can assess vendors on various criteria, including cost, quality, reliability, and even their commitment to values important to the nonprofit, like sustainability. This not only speeds up the selection process but also ensures a more objective and comprehensive evaluation, potentially uncovering cost-effective and innovative sourcing opportunities that might be overlooked manually.

AI also plays a pivotal role in contract management and negotiations. AI tools can analyze contract terms to ensure they align with the nonprofit's interests and project goals. They can also assist in negotiations by providing market insights, suggesting optimal pricing based on historical data, and even predicting the outcomes of negotiation strategies.

Furthermore, AI enhances the adaptability of procurement management. By continuously analyzing project progress and external market conditions, AI systems can provide real-time recommendations for procurement adjustments, ensuring that the procurement strategy stays aligned with dynamic project needs and external factors.

Budget management and cost control are also areas where AI can have a significant impact. AI can track expenditures in real-time, identify patterns in spending, and suggest cost-saving measures. It can even forecast future expenses, helping nonprofits manage their budgets more effectively and make informed decisions that maximize their resources' impact.

Incorporating AI into procurement management not only streamlines the process but also imbues it with a level of precision, foresight, and efficiency that traditional methods struggle to achieve. For nonprofits, where every resource counts, leveraging AI in procurement can lead to more successful projects, better resource utilization, and enhanced organizational credibility, ultimately amplifying their impact on the communities they serve.

Atmosphere Management

This less commonly cited but equally important aspect involves creating and maintaining a positive and supportive environment within the project team. A nurturing atmosphere encourages teamwork, innovation, and a high level of engagement among team members.

Incorporating AI into atmosphere management can significantly enhance the creation and maintenance of a positive project environment. AI-driven tools can analyze team communication patterns, identify stress indicators, and even suggest interventions to improve team dynamics and morale. For example, AI could analyze team meeting transcripts or communication channels to detect signs of conflict or disengagement, prompting leaders to take proactive steps to address these issues.

AI can also support the personalization of employee engagement strategies. By analyzing individual team member feedback and performance data, AI can offer tailored recommendations for recognition, professional development, and support, ensuring that each team member feels valued and understood. This individualized approach can boost morale and engagement, fostering a more cohesive and motivated team.

Moreover, AI can assist in monitoring the team's overall atmosphere by providing regular insights into team sentiment, collaboration levels, and engagement trends. This ongoing analysis can help leaders make informed decisions to cultivate a supportive and positive work environment, adapting strategies as the project evolves to maintain a high level of team morale.

AI's role in conflict resolution is another area of potential impact. By identifying early signs of disagreement or tension within the team, AI can prompt timely interventions, offering conflict resolution tools or suggesting when human mediation is necessary. This can help maintain a harmonious team atmosphere, ensuring that conflicts are resolved constructively and do not escalate into more significant issues.

In essence, integrating AI into Atmosphere Management offers a dynamic and data-driven approach to fostering a positive work environment. By leveraging AI's analytical capabilities, project leaders can gain deeper insights into team dynamics, tailor engagement strategies, and proactively address potential issues, ultimately creating a nurturing atmosphere that drives team success and project effectiveness.

CHAPTER 10

Marketing and Communication

The single biggest problem in communication is the illusion that it has taken place.[1]

—George Bernard Shaw

To make a difference, shed light on issues that matter to them, inform, and garner support, organizations in the nonprofit sector need to tell their stories. In the crowded space they operate in, effective storytelling is paramount for nonprofits to amplify their visibility and attract vital resources to fuel their engine. Marketing and communications in the nonprofit sector are not just about promoting an organization; they are about building meaningful connections, sharing compelling narratives, and mobilizing support for causes that matter. By strategically leveraging these tools, nonprofits can amplify their impact, garner the necessary resources, and engage a diverse array of stakeholders who play crucial roles in advancing their mission.

Increasing Visibility and Garnering Support

Compelling narratives lie at the heart of successful nonprofit communication strategies. They serve to humanize the organization's mission, making it relatable and inspiring to a diverse audience. By highlighting real-life stories of impact and showcasing the tangible outcomes of their initiatives, nonprofits can create a deeper connection with stakeholders.

Effective storytelling can evoke empathy and emotion, motivating individuals and entities to offer their support, whether through donations, volunteering, or advocacy efforts. But, in a landscape where limited resources must be allocated strategically, investing in storytelling and narrative creation can sometimes take a back seat.

Many nonprofits often face challenges in allocating resources to this aspect of their operations. In many cases, limited funding and competing priorities force organizations to prioritize mission-critical activities over communication and narrative-building efforts. The decision to invest in additional frontline staff, such as social workers, rather than hiring communication officers, is frequently made out of necessity. As a result, nonprofits may struggle to convey their impact effectively and attract the support they need to thrive.

However, the emergence of AI offers new opportunities for nonprofits to overcome this challenge. With AI, there is hope that financial constraints will no longer impede nonprofits' ability to tell their stories and attract support.

By leveraging AI-driven tools and techniques, nonprofits can create personalized, emotionally resonant narratives that resonate with their target audiences, ultimately driving greater engagement and support for their cause.

AI-powered tools can analyze vast amounts of data to identify impactful stories and trends that resonate with specific audiences. By understanding the preferences and interests of target supporters, AI can facilitate the creation of personalized and emotionally resonant narratives. This data-driven approach simplifies the drafting of messages and ensures that they are tailored to capture the attention and empathy of diverse stakeholders.

Additionally, AI's predictive analytics functions enable nonprofits to identify potential supporters and anticipate trends in communication strategies. By analyzing past engagement data and social media interactions, AI can predict which messages are most likely to resonate with specific demographics. This empowers nonprofits to tailor their communication efforts for maximum impact and support, ultimately enhancing their ability to attract resources and advance their mission.

Advocating for Issues

Shedding light on issues they are trying to tackle is part of the mandate of most nonprofit organizations. For this to happen, nonprofits need to advocate with passion and consistency for the causes and issues they care deeply about. The use of strategic messaging and awareness campaigns help nonprofits bring needed attention to critical social, environmental, or humanitarian issues that matter. By articulating the urgency and significance of their causes, nonprofits can influence public opinion, sway policy decisions, and mobilize collective action. Effective advocacy campaigns not only increase awareness, but they also contribute to shaping narratives that align with the sector values and objectives.

Limitations on percentages of funding that can be dedicated to advocacy campaigns on top of general financial limitations, and sometimes, the stringent rules that guide these types of activities can often discourage many nonprofits from embarking on consistent and time-consuming campaigns.

However, with AI, the era of automated advocacy campaigns is about to start. AI-driven automation tools can streamline the process of advocacy campaign management, including content creation, distribution, and targeted outreach. Not only by allowing the simplified crafting of powerful advocacy messages but by automating routine tasks, such as scheduling social media posts or sending personalized e-mails, nonprofits can free up valuable time and resources to focus on strategic advocacy efforts. This ensures that advocacy messages are consistently delivered across multiple channels, increasing visibility and engagement.

Personalized content recommendations that used to take time and a lot of capacity can now take place with simple clicks. AI algorithms can analyze supporter data to recommend personalized content, including stories, updates, and calls to action. And by tailoring communication to individual preferences, nonprofits can create a more engaging and relevant experience for each supporter. Personalization increases the likelihood of supporters actively participating and advocating for the cause.

Moreover, AI-powered natural language processing algorithms for policy analysis can assist nonprofits in analyzing policy documents, legislative texts, and public statements related to their advocacy issues. By extracting key insights and trends from large volumes of text data, AI can help nonprofits stay informed about policy changes and developments. This enables organizations to craft informed advocacy positions and effectively communicate their stance to stakeholders.

Add on top of that, tools for social media listening and sentiment analysis, and a small nonprofit can become a force to be reckoned with. New AI tools can monitor social media platforms to track conversations and sentiments related to the nonprofit's advocacy issues. By analyzing social media data in real-time, nonprofits are able to identify emerging trends, respond to public concerns, and engage with supporters proactively. This ensures that advocacy efforts remain relevant and responsive to the evolving needs and interests of stakeholders.

In conclusion, the integration of AI technologies into advocacy efforts holds great promise for nonprofit organizations. By leveraging automation, personalization, and advanced analytics, nonprofits can amplify their voices, maximize their impact, and drive meaningful change in the world. As we embrace this new era of AI-powered advocacy, nonprofits have the opportunity to revolutionize how they engage with supporters, influence policy, and advance their missions.

Informing and Engaging Stakeholders

Transparent and consistent communication is essential for keeping various stakeholders informed about a nonprofit's activities, values, and impact. Regular updates through newsletters, annual reports, and targeted communication campaigns ensure that supporters, beneficiaries, volunteers, and partners are aware of the organization's ongoing efforts. This transparency builds trust and credibility within the community, reinforcing the nonprofit's commitment to its mission. Clear communication also serves as a means to educate stakeholders on how they can access services, contribute, or get involved.

AI is now allowing interactivity and proactivity in the engagement process that were unseen before.

The implementation of AI-powered chatbots on websites and social media platforms for instance is allowing nonprofits to provide instant information and support to stakeholders. Chatbots can now answer queries, provide updates on ongoing initiatives, and guide individuals on how to get involved. This enhances transparency and accessibility, fostering a sense of engagement and shared purpose among stakeholders.

And the use of augmented reality (AR) and virtual reality (VR) experiences are enriching even further the engagement process. AI technologies can now enhance storytelling through immersive experiences like AR and VR. Nonprofits can use AI to create interactive content that allows supporters to experience the organization's mission firsthand. These immersive technologies can evoke powerful emotions, deepening connections with the cause and generating excitement among supporters.

In summary, AI can serve as a powerful ally for nonprofits in achieving their marketing and communications objectives. From personalized storytelling to predictive analytics and immediate engagement through virtual assistants, AI technologies contribute to building a more connected, informed, and enthusiastic community around the nonprofit's mission and impact.

Marketing and communications should always be key functions in the nonprofit sector. The skills, time, and resources needed to implement robust and effective marketing and communication strategies have made it very hard, until now, for many organizations in the nonprofit sector to accomplish these critical functions. But with the advent of AI, marketing and communications efforts of nonprofits can now be significantly enhanced to help them achieve their visibility, support, advocacy, and stakeholders engagement goals.

CHAPTER 11

Human Resources Management

In the past, the man has been first; in the future, the system must be first.

—**Frederick W. Taylor**

In the exhilarating race of achieving social impact, we often compare nonprofits to the sleek and powerful Formula 1 cars.

These organizations, like the finest cars on the track, are designed for high performance, driven by missions that demand speed, agility, and endurance. And who are the drivers? The dedicated individuals who work tirelessly within these nonprofits, steering these missions with skill and passion.

But even the best Formula 1 car, with the most skilled driver, requires a pit stop. This is where the vehicle is refueled, its tires changed, and any necessary adjustments made to ensure optimal performance.

In this chapter, we delve into the nuances of Human Resources Management (HRM) specifically tailored for the nonprofit sector. Our focus is on ensuring that your organization, your Formula 1 car, is always running at its best.

Human resources pose a critical dimension of limitation for nonprofits. Skilled personnel are essential for driving the success of social impact initiatives, yet attracting and retaining talent remains a formidable task. Many nonprofits, especially smaller organizations, face difficulties in offering competitive salaries and benefits, making it challenging to compete with other sectors for top-tier professionals. In the realm of talent acquisition, nonprofits often find themselves in direct competition with for-profit entities that may offer more lucrative compensation packages. The challenge of attracting skilled professionals to the nonprofit sector is exacerbated by the perception that these organizations may have limited career advancement opportunities or lack the financial stability for long-term employment.

The human resource struggle within nonprofits is further compounded by potential mismatches between the skills required for a particular program and the expertise of the recruited staff. This limitation can affect the overall efficacy of programs and place additional strain on existing personnel who may need to wear multiple hats to compensate for the lack of specialized support.

This scarcity of skilled personnel not only impacts the day-to-day operations of nonprofits but also hinders their capacity to adapt to evolving challenges and implement innovative solutions.

Frederick W. Taylor's quote, "In the past, the man has been first; in the future, the system must be first," offers a prescient view into the evolution of workplace dynamics, especially relevant from an HRM perspective in the age of AI.

Taylor, known for his principles of scientific management, advocated for efficiency and systematic work in industrial operations. Interpreted in the context of HRM, this quote suggests a shift from a traditional, human-centric approach to one where systems, processes, and technologies take precedence.

In modern HRM, particularly with the integration of AI, this shift becomes increasingly relevant. AI and automated systems are transforming how HR functions are performed. For instance, AI can handle repetitive tasks like payroll processing or resume screening, allowing HR professionals to focus on more strategic roles that require human judgment and empathy, such as employee relations and talent development.

However, Taylor's vision of putting the system first doesn't imply deprioritizing the human element. Instead, it's about leveraging systems and technologies like AI to enhance human work. In HRM, this means using AI to provide data-driven insights for better decision making, improving employee experiences through personalized learning and development programs, and creating more efficient workflows.

Moreover, in the future of work, where remote and flexible working arrangements are becoming more common, AI-driven systems facilitate collaboration and communication, helping maintain team cohesion and productivity regardless of physical location.

From an HRM standpoint, embracing Taylor's philosophy in the context of AI involves creating a balance. It's about designing systems and processes that enhance human capabilities and work experiences, rather than replacing or overshadowing the human aspect. The focus shifts to how systems and AI can augment human skills and contribute to a more efficient, effective, and fulfilling work environment.

Interpreting Taylor's quote through the lens of modern HRM and AI, it's not about choosing systems over people, but rather about harmonizing systems with human capabilities to create a more dynamic, efficient, and people-centered workplace. This approach acknowledges the value of systematic efficiency brought by AI, while also recognizing the irreplaceable qualities of human insight, creativity, and empathy in the hrm workplace.

What Do We Manage? Tasks, Skills, and Talent

A fundamental question: What exactly are we managing? The answer extends beyond just people. It encompasses the management of tasks, the development of skills, and the nurturing of talent. As illustrated in Figure 11.1 each of these components plays a vital role in building a successful organization, and with the advent of AI, managing these aspects has taken on a new dimension.

Managing Tasks: The Role of AI

In the dynamic world of organizational management, the effective allocation, execution, and monitoring of tasks stand as crucial pillars. As these tasks become increasingly complex and

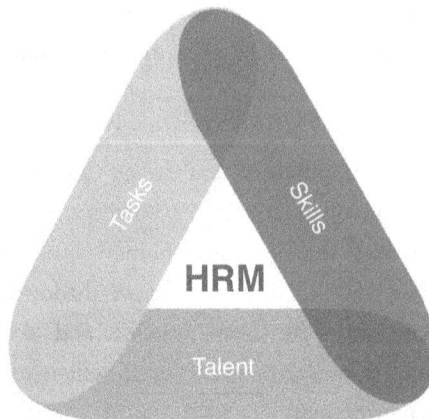

Figure 11.1 Three components of HRM

multifaceted, AI has stepped in as a transformative force, reshaping how these day-to-day activities are managed.

The integration of AI in task management is not just about automation; it's about enhancing the synergy between human capabilities and technological efficiency. AI's role in handling routine and repetitive tasks, such as scheduling, data entry, and responding to basic customer service inquiries, is well acknowledged. This automation plays a crucial part in streamlining processes, significantly boosting efficiency. However, the real power of AI lies in its ability to free up human employees to engage in more complex, strategic tasks. These are the kinds of tasks that necessitate critical thinking, creativity, and human insight—areas where AI serves as a support rather than a replacement.

As tasks within organizations evolve, becoming more intricate and interconnected, the necessity for a collaborative approach between AI and human intelligence becomes increasingly evident. AI-driven analytics, for instance, can assist in the prioritization of tasks. By analyzing data patterns and organizational needs, AI can provide recommendations on which tasks should be tackled first, ensuring that efforts are concentrated on areas with the highest impact or urgency. This not only enhances productivity but also ensures a more strategic allocation of human resources.

Moreover, as tasks grow in complexity, the integration of AI and human effort becomes a dance of balance and complementarity. For example, in problem-solving scenarios, AI can process and analyze vast amounts of data to identify potential solutions. However, the final decision making often requires human judgment, emotional intelligence, and ethical considerations—areas where AI is yet to match human capability.

In essence, the role of AI in managing tasks is evolving to meet the growing complexity of organizational demands. It's about creating an environment where AI and human employees work in tandem, each playing to their strengths. AI offers speed, accuracy, and data-processing capabilities, while human employees bring creativity, judgment, and strategic thinking to the table. Together, this partnership paves the way for higher productivity, smarter task management, and a more agile and responsive organization.

Developing Skills: AI's Contribution

The strength and adaptability of an organization significantly hinge on the continuous development of skills. As we navigate through an ever-changing world, the skill sets required for success and impact are in a state of constant evolution. This is where AI steps in, not just as a tool, but as a pivotal ally in ensuring that skills development keeps pace with these changes.

AI's role in skills development is multifaceted and increasingly crucial. With its ability to offer personalized and adaptive learning experiences, AI is redefining how training and development are approached. AI-driven training programs are adept at assessing individual learning styles and performance, allowing the content to be tailored to meet the specific needs of each employee. This personalized approach ensures that every team member receives training that resonates with them, leading to more effective learning outcomes and a more engaged learning experience.

The significance of AI in skills development extends beyond personalization. In a world where new technologies, methodologies, and best practices emerge regularly, keeping the workforce abreast of these changes is vital for a nonprofit's competitiveness and relevance. AI systems can continuously scan the external environment to identify emerging trends and required skill sets. By analyzing job market data, industry trends, and even internal performance metrics, AI can pinpoint skills gaps within the organization.

Once these gaps are identified, AI can recommend specific training and development initiatives. This might include online courses, workshops, or even in-house training sessions tailored to address these gaps. The proactive nature of this approach means that nonprofits are not merely reacting to skills deficits; they are anticipating and preparing for them.

Furthermore, as the required skills evolve, so does the need for continuous training and adjustments. AI plays a key role here by monitoring the effectiveness of existing training programs and suggest-ing modifications as needed. For instance, if an AI analysis reveals that certain skill sets are no longer as relevant or are being replaced by new ones, it can guide the organization in adjusting its training focus accordingly.

AI's contribution to skills development also lies in its ability to track and measure the impact of training over time. By analyzing changes in performance metrics pre- and post-training, AI can provide valuable insights into the effectiveness of different training programs. This not only helps in refining the approach to skills development but also ensures that investments in training yield tangible benefits.

The integration of AI into skills development processes is becoming indispensable for nonprofits. As the required skill sets for effective operation and impact continue to evolve, AI's role in identifying, addressing, and adapting to these changes is key. By leveraging AI for personalized, data-driven, and proactive skills development, nonprofits can ensure that their human capital is not just competent, but also resilient and prepared for the challenges of a dynamic world.

Nurturing Talent: Leveraging AI

Every individual possesses unique talents that, when nurtured and developed, can bring immense value to an organization. In the context of nonprofit organizations, where each role can significantly impact the overall mission, recognizing and cultivating these talents is crucial. AI is emerging as a key player in this arena, transforming how we identify, develop, and retain talent.

AI's contribution to talent management is multifaceted and increasingly impactful. Its capabilities extend from the initial stages of recruitment to the ongoing development and retention of staff.

In recruitment, AI algorithms are revolutionizing the way organiza-tions sift through applications. By analyzing vast numbers of resumes and applications, AI can efficiently identify candidates whose skills, experience, and attributes best match the job requirements. This process not only streamlines the recruitment process but also plays a significant role in minimizing unconscious biases. AI's objective analysis can lead to a more diverse and competent workforce, as it focuses solely on candidates' qualifications and potential fit with the organization's culture and needs.

For talent retention, AI tools offer an unprecedented ability to analyze employee engagement and satisfaction. By gathering and interpreting data from various sources—including surveys, performance metrics, and even informal feedback channels—AI can provide deep insights into what keeps employees motivated and committed to the organization. This understanding is vital for nonprofits seeking to maintain a passionate and dedicated team.

AI-driven analytics can highlight factors that contribute to employee satisfaction, such as work–life balance, recognition, and alignment with the organization's mission. These insights enable management to implement targeted strategies to boost morale and reduce turnover, ensuring that the organization retains its most valuable asset—its people.

Moreover, AI's role in career pathing marks a significant advancement in supporting professional growth and development. AI can analyze an individual's skills, performance history, and even their learning preferences to suggest potential career trajectories within the organization. It can identify the training and experiences needed for an employee to advance to the next level or to transition into different roles that align with their talents and interests.

By doing so, AI supports a culture of continuous learning and growth, where employees see a clear path for advancement and development. This not only benefits the employees but also aids the organization by ensuring that its team members are growing in their roles, staying engaged, and contributing to the nonprofit's mission in increasingly impactful ways.

The rise of AI in nurturing talent represents a significant evolution in the field of HRM. It transforms talent management from a largely reactive and intuition-based practice to a data-driven, strategic endeavor. AI's ability to uncover the potential in each individual and provide pathways for their growth not only enhances the individual's career but also contributes to the rise and evolution of human talent within the organization. This symbiotic relationship between AI and human potential is paving the way for nonprofits to achieve their mission through a skilled, motivated, and continuously evolving workforce.

Volunteer Management: The AI Revolution

In the world of nonprofit organizations, volunteers are the lifeblood that drives community initiatives and social change. Effectively managing these invaluable human resources is crucial, and this is where AI can play a transformative role.

Streamlining Volunteer Recruitment With AI

Volunteer recruitment is a critical first step in volunteer management, and it's an area where AI can bring about significant improvements. Traditional methods of volunteer recruitment often involve sifting through numerous applications manually, a process that can be both time-consuming and inefficient. AI revolutionizes this by using sophisticated algorithms to analyze the vast pool of potential volunteers. These algorithms are designed to match individuals' skills, interests, and availability with the specific needs of the nonprofit organization.

For example, if a nonprofit is organizing a community clean-up event, AI can identify volunteers who have shown interest in environmental causes, live in the vicinity, and are available on the scheduled dates. This level of precision in matching volunteers with opportunities ensures a much higher likelihood of a successful fit. Consequently, volunteers are more likely to have a fulfilling experience, as they are engaged in activities that resonate with their personal interests and skills sets. This efficient and targeted approach not only saves valuable administrative time but also plays a crucial role in enhancing the volunteer experience from the outset.

Personalized Volunteer Engagement

In volunteer engagement, AI brings a level of personalization that was previously unattainable for most nonprofits. Drawing parallels from consumer marketing, where AI is used to tailor experiences to individual preferences, nonprofits can apply similar technology to understand and engage with their volunteers. AI can analyze various data points from volunteers, such as their past volunteering activities, feedback, and interactions with the organization, to gain insights into their preferences and motivations.

This information enables nonprofits to create personalized communication and engagement strategies for each volunteer. For instance, a volunteer who frequently participates in educational programs might receive updates about upcoming tutoring sessions or educational fundraisers. Personalized emails, messages, and even volunteer opportunities can make volunteers feel more connected and valued, increasing their engagement and loyalty to the organization.

Moreover, this personalized approach extends to recognizing and appreciating volunteers' contributions. AI can track individual volunteer contributions and prompt timely recognition, whether through a thank-you note, a shout-out in a newsletter, or an invitation to a special appreciation event. This level of acknowledgment can significantly boost volunteer morale and reinforce their commitment to the nonprofit.

Optimizing Scheduling and Allocation of Tasks

The scheduling and allocation of tasks are critical components in volunteer management, often requiring a delicate balance to match volunteer availability with organizational needs. AI brings a level of efficiency and precision to this process that was previously unattainable. With AI-driven tools, nonprofits can automate much of the scheduling process, accommodating the individual availability of volunteers while also aligning this with the specific requirements and timelines of various tasks.

For instance, AI can analyze the availability data provided by volunteers and match it against the schedule of upcoming events or projects. If a large event is planned, the AI system can quickly identify which volunteers are available and have the skills necessary for specific roles within that event, whether it's logistics support, guest management, or on-site coordination. This automated matching and scheduling reduce the significant administrative burden that often falls on volunteer coordinators, allowing them to focus on higher-level engagement and strategy.

Moreover, AI's role in task allocation goes beyond mere scheduling. It can also assess the complexity and skills requirements of tasks and match them with volunteers' skills levels and preferences. This ensures that volunteers are not only available but also aptly suited for the tasks, leading to more effective and satisfying volunteer experiences.

Training and Development

Training and development are crucial in ensuring that volunteers are well-equipped to perform their roles effectively. AI is transforming this aspect of volunteer management by offering customized, scalable training solutions. AI-powered training platforms can tailor learning experiences to the specific roles and responsibilities of volunteers, factoring in their individual learning styles and progress.

For example, a volunteer taking on a leadership role in an event might receive AI-curated content focusing on team management, conflict resolution, and effective communication. These platforms can utilize various formats, from instructional videos and interactive modules to virtual simulations, providing a rich and engaging learning experience.

The adaptability of AI in training also means that it can continuously update training content based on the evolving needs of the organization and feedback from the volunteers. This ensures that the training material remains relevant, practical, and effective.

Furthermore, AI can track the progress of volunteers through their training modules, providing insights into areas where they excel or need further development. This allows for more targeted support and guidance, ensuring that volunteers are not just trained but are also continually developing their skills and capabilities.

Feedback and Improvement

In the dynamic field of volunteer management, the ethos of continuous improvement is integral. It's about constantly evolving and refining processes to better meet the needs of both the organization and its volunteers. Here, AI steps in as a crucial tool, facilitating a feedback loop that drives continuous improvement.

AI's capability to collect and analyze feedback from volunteers is a game-changer. Traditionally, feedback processes can be cumbersome and time-consuming, often resulting in a delay in action. However, AI can streamline this process, gathering feedback through various digital touchpoints like postevent surveys, regular check-ins, and interactive platforms.

Once collected, AI's advanced analytics come into play. It can sift through large volumes of feedback data, identifying key themes and patterns. For instance, AI might analyze survey responses to gauge overall volunteer satisfaction, pinpoint common challenges faced by volunteers, or highlight areas where volunteers feel particularly fulfilled.

With this data, AI can pinpoint specific areas in the volunteer program that need attention or improvement. This could range from operational aspects like the efficiency of the scheduling process to more subjective areas like the overall volunteer engagement strategy.

For example, if AI detects a recurring pattern of feedback regarding the need for more comprehensive training in a particular area, this insight can prompt an enhancement of the training program. Similarly, if volunteers express a desire for more flexible scheduling options, the organization can explore AI-driven solutions to accommodate this preference.

The next step is where the real value of AI in continuous improvement comes to the fore—implementing changes based on feedback and then monitoring the impact of these changes. AI can help track the effectiveness of new strategies or modifications made to the volunteer program. By comparing pre- and postchange feedback, AI can assess whether the adjustments have had the desired effect, whether that's increased volunteer satisfaction, improved performance, or better alignment with organizational goals.

This ongoing process of collecting feedback, analyzing it for actionable insights, implementing changes, and then reassessing ensures that the volunteer program remains dynamic, responsive, and aligned with the needs and expectations of its volunteers.

In conclusion, integrating AI into volunteer management offers a multitude of benefits. From streamlined recruitment and personalized engagement to efficient scheduling and continuous improvement, AI equips nonprofits with the tools they need to effectively manage their volunteers. In doing so, AI not only enhances the operational efficiency of volunteer programs but also significantly boosts the satisfaction and retention of these invaluable contributors.

CHAPTER 12

Measuring Impact

Evaluation and Learning

If you can't measure it, you can't manage it.[1]

—**Peter Drucker**

Can artificial intelligence (AI) help nonprofits measure and showcase their impact? The answer is a strong yes. Before exploring how AI facilitates this, it's crucial to understand why impact has become the currency in the nonprofit sector. Let's sit down for a moment and think about a decision many of us face when it comes to donating to charities. Picture two different organizations you could donate to: one spends a hefty 60 percent of its budget on overhead and administrative costs, while the other only spends 10 percent. At first glance, you might lean toward the second one, right? It seems they're putting more of your money directly toward their cause.

But, let's add a twist to our story. The first charity, despite its high overhead, is doing some pretty incredible work. They're delivering food and drinkable water to children in a developing country in Africa. That's a tough job with lots of challenges—think about the logistics, the safety measures, and the sheer effort it takes to get things done in such tough conditions.

On the other hand, our second charity, the one with the low overhead, is making sure kids from low-income families in Ottawa get toys for Christmas. That's a sweet and meaningful gesture, bringing smiles and joy to these children.

Now, does that make you rethink your choice? It's a bit of a head-scratcher, isn't it? The first charity's high overhead costs might not seem so outrageous when you consider the complexity and critical nature of their work. Meanwhile, the second charity, while being efficient with their funds, might not be meeting needs as crucial as providing essential nourishment and water.

Here's the takeaway from our little chat: when you're deciding where to put your hard-earned money, it's not just about how much a charity spends on overhead. It's also about the impact of their work. A high overhead might be a sign that a charity is tackling some really challenging issues, needing more resources to make a significant impact. On the flip side, a lower overhead doesn't always mean the work is less important, but it might not be as complex or demanding.

The concept of impact on the nonprofit sector, much like the role of currency in economics, is the pivotal measure of value and success. In this realm, impact is the *currency* that quantifies an organization's contribution to its mission. Integrating AI into the measurement of Social Return on Investment (SROI) offers a nuanced approach, similar to adapting a foreign currency in a domestic market. While SROI provides a metric for assessing nonfinancial value, incorporating AI can enhance its relevance and accuracy within the nonprofit context.

AI's capacity to analyze complex data sets enables a more sophisticated assessment of impact, considering both the broad societal changes and the nuanced individual transformations. This AI-enhanced SROI isn't just about assigning a numerical value to social impact; it's about understanding the depth and breadth of change, capturing insights that traditional methods might overlook. Nonprofits can then leverage these insights to refine their strategies, ensuring that their efforts are directed where they can make the most significant difference.

By adopting AI in impact measurement, nonprofits can develop a more contextual and dynamic understanding of their contributions. This approach aligns with the intrinsic goals of the sector, moving beyond the simple adaptation of business metrics to a more tailored, insightful evaluation of social and environmental value. AI not only helps in quantifying impact but also in narrating the stories behind the numbers, providing a comprehensive view of success and value in the nonprofit world.

The importance of measuring impact in the nonprofit sector is underscored by the famous adage of Peter Drucker: "If you can't measure it, you can't manage it." Recognizing this critical need, the development of a multidimensional model like ITCOS (Individual, Target group, Communities, Organizations, Society) is a significant advancement in the field. ITCOS, as it is illustrated in Figure 12.1 and Figure 12.2, with its focus on five distinct layers, offers a comprehensive approach to quantifying and understanding the impact of nonprofit activities.

By dissecting impact into these layers—Individual, Target Group, Communities, Organizations, and Society—ITCOS provides a structured and nuanced framework for evaluation. This methodology ensures that the assessment isn't just one-dimensional or superficial but instead captures the varied and complex effects of a nonprofit's work. Each layer represents a different level at which impact occurs:

- **Individual:** Measuring changes in individual behaviors, skills, and attitudes.
- **Target Group:** Assessing the impact on specific groups the project is designed to benefit.
- **Communities:** Evaluating broader effects on community dynamics and well-being.
- **Organizations:** Understanding the influence on organizational structures, processes, and capabilities.
- **Society:** Gauging wider societal shifts and contributions to social change.

By integrating the ITCOS model alongside AI technology, organizations can significantly elevate their capability to track, measure, and interpret their impact. AI enhances this model by providing deeper, data-driven insights that inform strategic planning and operational enhancements. This integration aligns with the principle that meticulous and precise measurement, powered by AI's analytical prowess, is crucial for managing and amplifying the effectiveness of nonprofit initiatives. AI's role in this context ensures that organizations not only quantify their impact accurately but

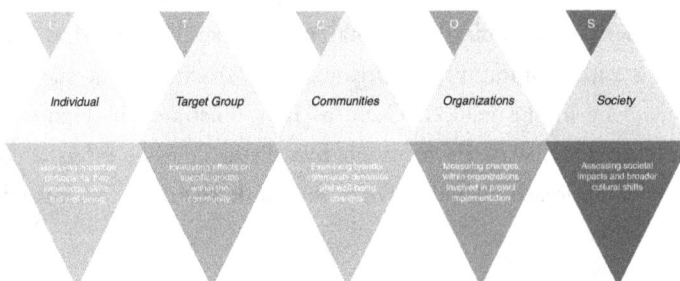

Figure 12.1 ITCUS impact measurement

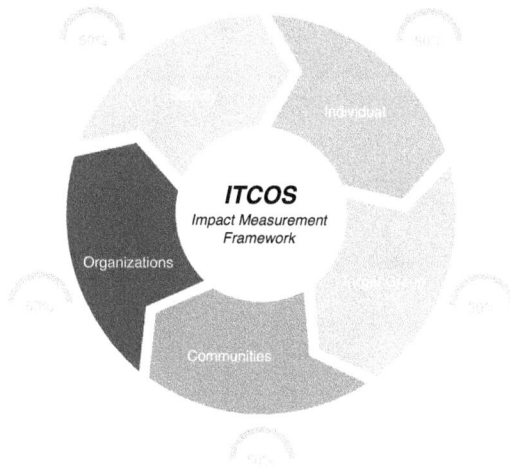

Figure 12.2 ITCUS *impact measurement framework*

also leverage these insights to make informed decisions, optimize operations, and ensure their initiatives make a substantial and enduring difference in their focus areas.

In our quest to enhance impact measurement within the nonprofit sector, we've integrated AI to refine our approach, employing customized quantitative metrics tailored for each organization. Utilizing AI, we analyze data on a 0 to 100 scale across the five layers of the ITCOS model, providing a nuanced, AI-enriched framework for comprehensive evaluation.

In the Individual Layer, AI aids in analyzing the direct impact on individuals, measuring changes in knowledge, skills, attitudes, and well-being. AI algorithms help interpret complex data sets, where, for example, a score of 70 signifies substantial individual improvement due to our interventions, pinpointing specific areas influenced by AI's deep insights.

At the Target Group Layer, AI enhances our metrics to assess the impact on specific groups. It processes variables like employment rates and educational achievements, providing a nuanced understanding of the impact. If a group scores 50, AI helps us delve deeper into the data, identifying precise improvement avenues or successes.

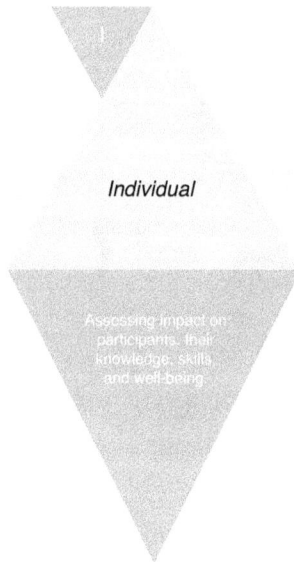

Figure 12.3

In the Communities Layer, AI's role extends to evaluating broader community impact. It analyzes trends in community engagement and economic development, where a score like 80, informed by AI's comprehensive analysis, reflects significant community advancements.

For the Organizations Layer, we leverage AI to gauge the impact on related organizations, assessing aspects like growth and efficiency. AI's capability to process vast organizational data aids in uncovering insights behind a score of 30, guiding targeted strategies to enhance organizational capacities.

Lastly, at the Society Layer, AI is pivotal in assessing societal impact. It evaluates wide-ranging effects like policy changes and societal attitudes, where a high score of 90 is backed by AI's robust analysis, highlighting our substantial contribution to societal progress. Through AI's power, our impact measurement transcends traditional boundaries, offering a dynamic, in-depth perspective of our influence across multiple layers.

Incorporating AI into this structured approach enhances our ability to capture a detailed and comprehensive picture of our impact within the nonprofit sector. By employing AI to quantify our achievements and identify areas for growth, we can make more informed

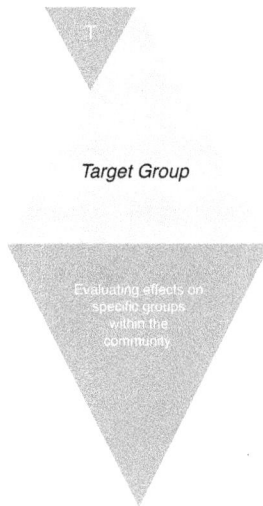

Figure 12.4

and strategic decisions, set achievable goals, and persistently aim for enhanced effectiveness in our initiatives. AI's advanced analytics and data processing capabilities provide deep insights into our performance, enabling a nuanced understanding of our impact across various dimensions.

This AI-enhanced method not only bolsters our internal understanding but also empowers us to articulate our successes and challenges more transparently and compellingly to our stakeholders. By leveraging AI to analyze and present our data, we can offer stakeholders a clearer and more data-driven view of our impact, reinforcing their trust and engagement with our organization. Ultimately, this approach ensures that our efforts are not just about meeting targets but about creating meaningful, measurable, and sustainable change, with AI serving as a critical tool in our ongoing journey toward greater impact and efficacy.

Individual Level Impact

In our framework, measuring impact at the individual level (Figure 12.3) is a critical component that focuses on assessing the changes in the lives of individuals directly influenced by our programs. This level of

Figure 12.5

measurement is both nuanced and deeply personal, as it revolves around the specific experiences and transformations of individuals.

To measure individual impact, we primarily rely on a blend of quantitative and qualitative metrics. Quantitative data might include metrics such as skill improvement scores, rates of employment following participation in a program, or educational achievements. For instance, we might track the percentage increase in employment among participants of a job training program.

Qualitative measures, on the other hand, are equally important. These often involve collecting personal stories and testimonials, which provide deeper insights into how our programs have affected individuals' lives. Surveys and interviews are key tools here, designed to capture changes in personal attitudes, self-esteem, and life satisfaction.

AI plays a transformative role in enhancing our ability to measure individual-level impact. One significant application of AI is in the analysis of large volumes of qualitative data. AI-powered text analysis tools can process thousands of survey responses or interview transcripts, identifying common themes and sentiments more efficiently and accurately than manual analysis. This helps us understanding the nuanced changes in individuals' lives that our programs facilitate.

AI can also aid in predictive analysis. By analyzing historical data, AI algorithms can predict the likely impact of certain programs on individuals. This predictive capability is invaluable in program design and refinement, allowing us to tailor our initiatives more closely to the needs of our target individuals.

Furthermore, AI can assist in personalizing interventions. By analyzing individual data points, AI can help identify the specific needs of each participant, enabling us to offer more personalized support. For example, in an educational program, AI can recommend specific learning paths for each student based on their learning style and progress.

Measuring impact at the individual level is a complex but essential part of our work. By combining traditional data collection methods with the power of AI, we can gain a more comprehensive understanding of our impact. This approach not only improves the accuracy of our impact measurement but also guides us in enhancing the effectiveness of our programs, ensuring that we make a meaningful difference in the lives of individuals we serve.

Target Group Level Impact

At the target group level (Figure 12.4), our focus shifts to understanding the extent of our reach among potential beneficiaries. This measurement is crucial in assessing how effectively we are serving the intended population, such as newcomers in a community. The target group level impact essentially quantifies the proportion of the potential beneficiaries that our programs successfully engage and serve.

The primary metric in this level of impact measurement is the percentage of potential beneficiaries reached by our programs. For instance, if there are 10,000 newcomers in a community and our program serves 2,000, our target group level impact would be calculated as 20 percent. This straightforward percentage offers a clear and quantifiable measure of our reach and effectiveness in addressing the needs of the target group.

In addition to the percentage metric, we also consider the depth of the impact on the target group. This involves understanding not just how many individuals we serve, but also how significantly our programs

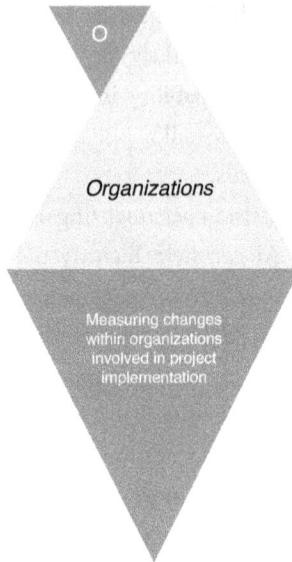

Figure 12.6

impact their lives. For this, we might assess improvements in quality of life, access to resources, or other specific indicators relevant to the target group.

AI can significantly enhance our ability to measure and understand target group level impact. AI's capabilities in data processing and analysis can provide a more nuanced understanding of our reach and effectiveness. One key application of AI in this context is in data aggregation and analysis. AI systems can efficiently process large data sets to provide insights into the demographics of the individuals we serve. By analyzing this data, we can determine whether we are effectively reaching all segments within the target group or if there are underserved subgroups that require more attention.

AI can also assist in predictive modeling. By analyzing existing data, AI algorithms can predict future trends in the needs and numbers of the target group. This information is invaluable for strategic planning, helping us to anticipate changes and adapt our programs accordingly. Moreover, AI can enhance the accuracy of our impact assessments. Through machine learning algorithms, we can analyze patterns and outcomes of our programs, identifying the most effective strategies and areas for improvement. This leads to more informed decision making and program development.

Measuring target group level impact is essential for understanding our reach and efficacy in serving our intended beneficiaries. With the aid of AI, we can not only measure this impact more accurately but also gain deeper insights that guide our efforts. By continually refining our approach based on these insights, we can improve our programs and ensure that a higher percentage of the target group benefits from our services.

Community Level Impact

When evaluating impact at the community level (Figure 12.5), our approach broadens to encompass the collective changes and benefits that our programs bring to entire communities. This level of measurement is crucial for understanding the broader social, economic, and cultural shifts that result from our interventions, and how these shifts contribute to the overall well-being and development of the community.

Measuring impact at the community level involves a variety of metrics that collectively paint a picture of the changes within a

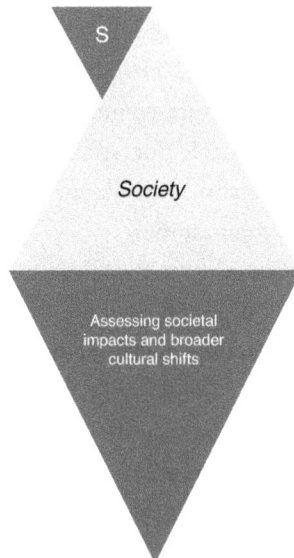

Figure 12.7

community. These metrics can include economic indicators such as local employment rates or business growth, social indicators like community cohesion or crime rates, and cultural indicators such as the preservation or evolution of local traditions and practices.

For instance, if a program is aimed at economic development, we might measure our impact by the increase in local employment or new business establishments. If the focus is on social well-being, we could look at changes in community engagement, reductions in crime rates, or improvements in public health.

In assessing these changes, both the scale (how widespread the impact is) and the depth (how significant the changes are) are considered. This dual focus helps us understand not just the extent of our impact but also its meaningfulness and sustainability. AI offers powerful tools to enhance the measurement and understanding of community-level impact. AI can process and analyze large sets of data from various sources, providing a comprehensive view of the community and the changes occurring within it.

One significant application of AI in this context is in the analysis of social and economic trends. By processing data from sources like surveys, social media, economic reports, and government databases, AI can identify patterns and trends that might not be immediately apparent. This helps in understanding the broader impact of our programs on the community. AI can also assist in predictive analytics, enabling us to forecast future community needs and trends. This predictive capacity is invaluable for strategic planning, allowing us to proactively design programs that address emerging challenges and opportunities within the community.

Furthermore, AI-driven geospatial analysis can provide insights into how impacts vary across different parts of the community. This can help in identifying areas that are benefiting more and those that might need additional attention, ensuring that our programs are equitable and inclusive. Measuring impact at the community level is essential for understanding the broader implications of our work. By incorporating AI into our measurement strategies, we can gain deeper and more accurate insights into the changes occurring within communities. This approach not only enhances the precision of our impact assessment but also guides us in making more informed decisions, ultimately leading to more effective and beneficial community-focused programs.

Organization Level Impact

At the organization level (Figure 12.6), our focus shifts to understanding the impact of our programs on the organizations involved, including our own. This measurement is essential to gauge how our initiatives contribute to the growth, efficiency, and effectiveness of organizations, which, in turn, influences their ability to create positive change.

Methods for Measuring Organization Level Impact

To measure impact at the organization level, we employ a range of metrics that reflect organizational health and capabilities. These metrics might include:

- **Capacity Building:** Assessing improvements in organizational capacity, such as increased staff skills, better infrastructure, or enhanced technological capabilities.
- **Efficiency and Productivity:** Measuring changes in operational efficiency, such as reduced costs, streamlined processes, or improved service delivery.
- **Growth and Sustainability:** Evaluating indicators of organizational growth, like expanded services, increased funding, or a larger beneficiary base. Sustainability metrics, such as the diversification of funding sources or long-term strategic planning, are also crucial.
- **Impact on Staff and Volunteers:** Understanding changes in staff and volunteer engagement, satisfaction, and turnover rates. A positive impact here often translates to better organizational performance.

These metrics provide a comprehensive view of the organizational changes and improvements resulting from our programs. By assessing both internal (e.g., staff capacity) and external (e.g., service delivery) aspects, we can obtain a holistic understanding of our impact on organizations.

AI can significantly augment our ability to measure and analyze organization-level impact. AI's capacity for data processing, analysis, and predictive modeling offers several advantages:

- **Data-Driven Insights:** AI can process vast amounts of organizational data, from operational metrics to staff feedback, providing deep insights into organizational health and areas for improvement.
- **Predictive Analysis:** AI algorithms can predict future organizational needs and challenges based on current and historical data. This predictive capability helps in strategic planning and proactive decision making.
- **Process Optimization:** AI can identify inefficiencies in organizational processes and suggest optimizations. This includes automating routine tasks, thereby freeing up resources for more strategic activities.
- **Enhanced Performance Monitoring:** Continuous monitoring of key performance indicators using AI tools allows for real-time assessment and quicker response to emerging issues or opportunities.

Measuring impact at the organization level is crucial for ensuring that our programs contribute effectively to the strength and sustainability of the organizations involved. By leveraging AI in our measurement strategies, we can gain a more nuanced and accurate understanding of this impact. Such insights not only drive improvements within our own organization but also enhance our capacity to support and collaborate with partner organizations, collectively amplifying our ability to create positive change.

Society Level Impact

Measuring and demonstrating the social impact of a project is a crucial aspect, especially in the context of securing government grants.

Governments typically prioritize funding for projects that promise the highest societal benefits, making it essential for organizations to effectively quantify and communicate the impact of their initiatives. This involves not only showcasing the direct outcomes and benefits for targeted groups and communities but also illustrating the broader societal changes such as policy influence, economic improvements, and cultural shifts. A robust impact assessment, therefore, becomes a key factor in justifying the value of a project and securing essential government support, driving forward initiatives that have a profound and positive effect on society.

With societal impact measurement (Figure 12.7), we delve into understanding how our initiatives bring about transformative changes across various facets of society. This level of assessment is complex, as it encompasses a broad spectrum of changes, including policy reforms, economic shifts, cultural evolutions, and environmental sustainability. The goal is to capture the deeper, long-term effects of our work on society, painting a picture of how we are contributing to positive societal transformation.

At this level, our approach involves assessing the influence of our programs on public policy, where we look at the adoption of new legislation or shifts in government priorities that align with our mission. The economic impact is another crucial aspect, where we examine indicators such as job creation, GDP growth, and market dynamics. Equally important is measuring cultural and social shifts, where we gauge changes in societal values, practices, and public attitudes, providing insights into how societal norms are evolving. Environmental sustainability forms a key part of our assessment too, focusing on the impact on natural resource management, pollution levels, and biodiversity conservation.

AI significantly enhances our ability to measure and analyze societal impacts. AI's capability in processing vast amounts of data from various sources, including social media, policy documents, and environmental reports, enables a comprehensive view of societal impacts. Predictive analytics, a forte of AI, allows us to foresee the long-term effects of our initiatives, aiding in strategic planning. AI's proficiency in sentiment analysis helps in understanding shifts in public opinion and cultural norms, providing a window into the societal transformation underway. In environmental sustainability, AI's role extends to monitoring and predicting environmental changes, crucial for assessing our ecological footprint and contributions to sustainability.

The task of measuring societal impact is integral to our mission of driving positive change. By incorporating AI into our measurement strategies, we not only enhance the accuracy of our assessments but also gain profound insights into how society is transforming. This data-driven approach enables us to continually adapt our strategies, ensuring that our efforts lead to meaningful and sustainable changes in society.

CHAPTER 13

Ethical Considerations and Responsible AI

Artificial Intelligence is progressing. And if we are not careful, it could become a Trojan horse for a single premise: the imposition of a one-size-fits-all approach to ethical decision-making.

—**Emmanuel R. Goffi, PhD**

Welcome to a super interesting and important topic in our high-tech world: AI Ethics. Emmanuel Goffi, a big name in this field, throws light on something we really need to think about. He's worried that as AI gets smarter and more a part of our lives, we might start seeing it make decisions based on a one-size-fits-all idea of what's right and wrong. But, hey, we all know life's not that simple. People are different, and what's right in one place might not be in another.

So, in this chapter, we're going to introduce how AI is changing things and what it means to use it in a way that's good for everyone. We'll look at big questions like how to make AI fair for all, how to keep it transparent (so we know how it's making decisions), and how to protect our privacy when AI is all around us.

We've got some cool stories and examples to share about how folks are working to keep AI on the right track. It's all about making sure it's used in ways that respect everyone's values and rights. So, come along on this journey with us through the world of AI ethics. It's not just about tech stuff; it's about shaping a future that's good for all of us.

Emmanuel Goffi's concerns about AI ethics are far from solitary. In the world of journalism, a field increasingly intertwined with AI, similar apprehensions are surfacing. A recent report from Euro News, based on findings from the London School of Economics (LSE)'s JournalismAI project, highlights this growing unease. The report reveals that while a majority of news organizations around the globe are now incorporating AI in various aspects of their operations, over 60 percent of the respondents are worried about the ethical implications of this integration.

This concern, stemming from the 105 news and media organizations surveyed across 46 countries between April and July 2023, underscores a broader, industrywide dilemma. While AI offers vast potential for enhancing journalistic work, from automating routine tasks to aiding in complex investigative reporting, it also brings forth ethical challenges. Issues like algorithmic bias, editorial integrity, and the transparency of AI-driven processes are at the forefront of these concerns. This global survey paints a picture of an industry grappling with the dualities of AI adoption—eager to embrace its advantages but cautious of its ethical ramifications.

An Interesting Case by WHO

The World Health Organization (WHO) has recently (May 16, 2023) raised significant concerns about the ethical implications of employing AI, particularly large language models like ChatGPT, Bard, and Bert, in the health care sector. As these AI technologies rapidly integrate into health care systems, WHO underscores the need for a cautious and ethical approach to their deployment.

One of the primary concerns raised by WHO is the potential for inherent biases in AI systems. Since AI models are trained on existing data, there's a risk that any biases present in the training data can be perpetuated and amplified by the AI. This can lead to skewed or unfair outcomes, particularly in sensitive areas like health care, where such biases can have serious implications for patient care and treatment outcomes.

Another significant worry is the accuracy and reliability of the information provided by AI systems. In health care, decisions often have life-or-death consequences, making it crucial that the information and recommendations provided by AI are accurate and reliable. The WHO cautions that without proper oversight and rigorous testing, AI systems could inadvertently provide misleading or incorrect health information, potentially endangering patient safety.

Data privacy is a paramount concern in health care. The WHO highlights the risk associated with the use of AI in handling sensitive health data. There is a potential threat to patient privacy if AI systems are not designed with stringent data protection measures. Additionally, there are concerns regarding the consent process for the use of personal health data in training and operating these AI models.

The potential misuse of AI to spread disinformation is another ethical concern. In the context of health care, the spread of false or misleading information can have serious public health implications. The WHO emphasizes the need for measures to prevent the misuse of AI in disseminating health-related disinformation.

In light of these concerns, the WHO advocates for the implementation of ethical frameworks and governance in the development and use of AI in health care. This includes adherence to principles like transparency, accountability, and public engagement. It is crucial that AI developments in health care are guided by ethical considerations that prioritize human well-being and safety.

The WHO's stance serves as a crucial reminder of the ethical challenges posed by the integration of AI in health care. It underscores the need for a balanced approach that harnesses the benefits of AI while mitigating risks and safeguarding ethical standards. The organization's concerns highlight the importance of developing AI in a manner that is not only technologically advanced but also ethically responsible, ensuring that AI serves as a tool for enhancing health care delivery and patient outcomes in an equitable and safe manner.

Understanding AI Ethics in Business

In his insightful article titled "Employees 'unsure' of company ethics guidelines for AI," Steph Brown sheds light on a significant issue in the contemporary corporate landscape—the apparent gap in employees' awareness and understanding of their companies' ethics guidelines concerning General AI (Gen AI). The findings from Deloitte's second annual report on the State of Ethics and Trust in Technology serve as a crucial focal point for this discussion.

The report's findings are quite revealing, with more than half (56%) of respondents indicating either a lack of Gen AI-specific ethics guidance in their companies or an unawareness of such guidelines. This statistic is alarming, considering the rapidly increasing integration of AI technologies in various business operations and decision-making processes.

The implementation and understanding of AI ethics are paramount in ensuring the responsible use of technology. AI systems, especially Gen AI, have far-reaching implications that can affect not only business outcomes but also ethical considerations like fairness, privacy, and accountability. The lack of clear guidelines or awareness among employees suggests a significant oversight in corporate governance and risk management.

This gap in awareness and guidelines can lead to several challenges. Without a clear ethical framework, employees might use AI technologies in ways that could inadvertently perpetuate biases, invade privacy, or make unaccountable decisions. Moreover, it could lead to a mistrust of AI technologies among employees and stakeholders, hampering their effective and beneficial use.

Brown's article emphasizes the need for companies to proactively develop and communicate clear, specific guidelines on the ethical use of AI. This involves not just drafting policies but also ensuring that employees at all levels are educated and aware of these guidelines. Regular training sessions, workshops, and accessible resources can help in embedding ethical AI use in the company culture.

The findings highlighted by Steph Brown in his article point to a crucial need for increased focus on AI ethics in the corporate world. As AI continues to evolve and become more ingrained in business processes, companies must take concerted steps to ensure that all employees are equipped with the knowledge and guidelines needed to use AI responsibly and ethically. This not only safeguards against potential risks but also maximizes the technology's benefits in a way that aligns with ethical and societal values.

As the digital landscape continues to evolve and expand its influence in our lives, a new and essential service is emerging, epitomized by the innovative work of Digital Ethicists, a French company. This forward-thinking enterprise is dedicated to guiding organizations in integrating ethical considerations into their digital activities. Recognizing the profound impact that digital technologies, especially AI, have on society, Digital Ethicists works to ensure that companies not only harness these technologies for progress and efficiency but also do so in a manner that is responsible, transparent, and aligned with ethical principles. Their approach involves helping organizations navigate the complex terrain of digital ethics, from data privacy and AI fairness to responsible innovation and beyond. By offering this crucial support, Digital Ethicists plays a pivotal role in shaping a digital future that is not just technologically advanced but also morally grounded and socially responsible.

Ethical Frameworks

Let's talk about popular ethical frameworks and how they can be related to AI. Think of these frameworks as a set of guidelines or rules that help us decide what's right and what's wrong, especially when dealing with tricky situations. In the world of ethics, especially with AI, there are a few key frameworks that people often talk about. Let's break them down:

Utilitarianism: This one's all about doing the most good for the most people. Imagine you're programming an AI to help with city traffic. Using utilitarianism, you'd want your AI to make decisions that help the most drivers get where they're going quickly and safely.

Deontology: This framework is like having a strict rulebook. It says there are some things you should and shouldn't do, no matter what. So, if you're creating an AI, deontology would mean making sure it always respects people's privacy, no matter what good it might do by bending the rules.

Virtue Ethics: Here, it's all about character. It's like asking, "What would a really good, wise person do?" So, if your AI is helping make decisions in a hospital, virtue ethics would want it to be compassionate and fair, just like the best doctors.

Care Ethics: This one focuses on relationships and caring for others. It's about empathy and understanding. If you're designing an AI for a school, care ethics would guide you to make sure the AI is supportive and kind to students.

Contractarianism: This framework is like making a deal or an agreement. It's about what rules people would agree to live by for everyone's benefit. In AI, this could mean creating systems that everybody, including the people who might be affected by the AI, would think are fair and just.

Existential Ethics: A bit philosophical, this one's about making choices that are authentic and true to oneself. For AI, it's a bit tricky, but it would mean creating AI that helps people make decisions that are genuinely good for their own lives.

Each of these frameworks offers a different way to look at tough questions and helps guide us in making ethical decisions, especially when it comes to technology like AI. It's like having a toolbox—depending on the job, you might need a different tool. In ethics, depending on the situation, a different framework might be the best fit!

How About Nonprofits

In the world of nonprofits, where every resource counts and the impact is paramount, the advent of AI presents both extraordinary opportunities and significant ethical challenges. As these organizations increasingly turn to AI to enhance efficiency, reach, and impact, understanding and addressing the ethical dimensions of this technology becomes crucial.

For nonprofits, AI can be a game-changer. From personalized donor engagement and predictive analytics for more effective fundraising strategies to AI-driven program evaluation and enhanced service delivery, the potential is vast. AI can help nonprofits do more with less, reaching more people, solving more complex problems, and making a bigger impact.

However, this bright promise is not without its shadows. One of the primary concerns is data ethics. Nonprofits often handle sensitive information, and ensuring the privacy and security of this data when using AI is paramount. There's also the risk of biases in AI algorithms that could lead to unfair or discriminatory outcomes, whether in donor profiling, beneficiary selection, or community outreach efforts.

Another ethical challenge lies in transparency and accountability. As AI systems can be complex and opaque, ensuring that decisions made by or with the aid of AI are transparent and explainable is essential.

This is especially important for maintaining trust among stakeholders—donors, beneficiaries, and the public.

The digital divide poses another ethical concern. As AI technology is more accessible to well-resourced nonprofits, there's a risk of widening the gap between larger organizations and smaller, community-based ones. This could inadvertently lead to an uneven playing field where the benefits of AI are not equitably distributed.

To navigate these challenges, nonprofits need to forge a responsible path forward. This involves developing and adhering to ethical guidelines for AI use, which include principles of fairness, transparency, privacy, and accountability. Engaging with stakeholders—from tech developers to the communities they serve—in the development and deployment of AI solutions is crucial.

Training and education are also key. Nonprofit leaders and staff need to be equipped with the knowledge to make informed decisions about using AI in their operations. This includes understanding both the potential and the limitations of AI, and where it can or should not be applied.

In conclusion, as nonprofits embrace the potential of AI, they must also navigate its ethical landscape with care. By prioritizing ethical considerations and engaging in thoughtful, inclusive discussions about the use of AI, nonprofits can harness this powerful technology to not only enhance their operations but also uphold their values and mission. The journey of integrating AI into the nonprofit sector is not just about technological adoption; it's about ensuring that this adoption aligns with the core ethos of social good and responsibility.

CHAPTER 14

Final Considerations and Looking Forward

The best way to predict the future is to invent it.

—Alan Key

This book, while not crafted by AI experts, serves as a gateway to demystify and introduce the transformative power of AI. Our aim was to provide you, the reader, with an accessible perspective on this formidable yet sometimes daunting tool. What we hope to instill is a sense of curiosity about the myriad possibilities AI holds—the potential to be a force for good within your community, whatever that community may be.

AI and Human Harmony

AI possesses the remarkable ability to empower nonprofits in overcoming long standing challenges, particularly the pervasive knowledge and resource gaps that have historically hindered the sector's full potential. The nonprofit sector is brimming with organizations driven by noble causes and aspirations, yet it has grappled with limitations stemming from a lack of access to cutting-edge technologies and data-driven insights.

Imagine a world where AI and humans team up like superheroes in a comic book, working hand in hand to tackle big problems and help communities grow stronger. In this future, AI isn't just a tool that people use; it's more like a friendly robot sidekick that helps out in all sorts of ways, big and small.

In this world, when a natural disaster strikes, like a big storm or an earthquake, AI systems quickly figure out where help is needed the most. They work with rescue teams to save people and make sure they have what they need, like food, water, and a safe place to stay. It's like having a supersmart helper that can see the big picture and the tiny details, all at once.

But it's not just about dealing with emergencies. Every day, in schools, hospitals, and cities, AI is there like a helpful neighbor. In schools, AI helps teachers understand what each student needs, making learning more fun and interesting. In hospitals, it helps doctors figure out the best way to make people feel better. And in cities, AI helps everything run smoothly, from traffic lights to water systems, making life easier and safer for everyone.

Now, imagine AI systems that can talk to each other, sharing what they learn and working together to come up with even better ways to help. It's like a network of friends, each with its own skills, teaming up to make the world a better place. They could help scientists discover new cures for diseases, help farmers grow more food, and even help us take better care of our planet.

In this future, AI is like a new member of the community, one that brings its own unique abilities to the table. Together, humans and AI can build a world where everyone has the support they need, where communities are strong, and where the future is bright and full of possibilities.

By delving into the world of AI, nonprofits can unlock new avenues for innovation and efficiency. AI's capacity to automate routine tasks liberates valuable human resources, enabling nonprofits to redirect their efforts toward more strategic and impactful endeavors. Through data analytics, AI equips organizations with the means to make informed decisions, tailor interventions to specific community needs, and enhance the overall effectiveness of their initiatives.

Moreover, AI acts as a catalyst for bridging the knowledge gap within the Nonprofit sector. It facilitates access to critical information, best practices, and innovative solutions that might have eluded organizations in the past. This democratization of knowledge empowers nonprofits of varying sizes to operate on a more level playing field, fostering a culture of collaboration, learning, and continuous improvement.

In essence, this book serves as an invitation to explore the untapped potential of AI in the Nonprofit sector. It beckons readers to envision a future where technological advancements amplify the impact of nonprofit organizations, enabling them to break free from the constraints of the past and fully realize their capacity to create positive change within communities. Through this exploration, we aspire to inspire a newfound confidence in harnessing AI as a tool not just for innovation but as a driving force for social good.

Tailored AI for Nonprofits

Nonprofit organizations have often been characterized as cautious adopters of new technology, not due to a lack of adventurous spirit or imagination but rather a result of resource constraints. The limited time and efforts of these organizations must remain concentrated on the essential functions of delivering services to their clients. The day-to-day operations absorb a significant portion of these scarce resources, leaving little room for experimentation, trial and error, or the adoption of new tools and processes—luxuries that seem unaffordable in the face of pressing service delivery needs.

AI for nonprofits does share some technological underpinnings with AI for businesses, yet the application, focus, and end goals diverge significantly due to the distinct nature of nonprofit organizations. While businesses primarily harness AI to boost profitability and efficiency, nonprofits leverage AI to amplify their impact, focusing on social and individual outcomes rather than financial gains.

In the nonprofit sector, AI is customized to align with the organization's mission-centric objectives. For instance, AI can help nonprofits in donor segmentation, not just to increase donations but to build meaningful relationships with donors, understanding their motivations and engagement preferences. This nuanced approach helps nonprofits to foster a community of supporters aligned with their mission, rather than just focusing on the monetary aspect.

Moreover, AI in nonprofits is often geared toward enhancing operational efficiency, but with the end goal of maximizing impact. For example, AI-powered tools can optimize resource allocation, ensuring that the maximum possible resources are directed toward program delivery and impact creation, rather than profit maximization. This includes optimizing routes for delivering aid, predicting areas of need, or identifying the most effective interventions in a given context.

Another distinct application of AI in nonprofits is in measuring and evaluating impact, which is the primary performance parameter for these organizations. AI can process vast amounts of data to assess the effectiveness of various programs and initiatives, helping nonprofits to understand their impact on the community and make data-driven decisions to enhance their efforts. This could involve analyzing trends in community health, education levels, or other key indicators over time.

Furthermore, AI can assist nonprofits in storytelling and advocacy, turning data into compelling narratives that showcase the organization's achievements and the significance of their work. This is crucial for nonprofits to secure funding, engage the community, and influence policy.

In summary, while AI for businesses and nonprofits might utilize similar tools, the focus for nonprofits is distinctly on maximizing social good and impact. The currency in the nonprofit sector is the positive change and benefits delivered to individuals and communities, guiding how AI technologies are applied and evaluated in this context.

AI as a Game-Changer

In this context, AI emerges as a beacon of possibility, a catalyst for change that transcends the traditional barriers faced by nonprofits. AI will bring enhanced efficiency, deeper insights, and greater impact to nonprofits. It will streamline operations, automate repetitive tasks, and optimize resource allocation, allowing organizations to focus more on their mission-driven work. AI will also provide advanced analytics, offering a deeper understanding of donor behavior, program effectiveness, and community needs, enabling more informed decision making. Furthermore, AI will amplify the impact of nonprofits by enabling personalized engagement strategies, improving intervention outcomes, and expanding the reach of their programs, ultimately fostering a more significant positive change in the communities they serve.

The hope is that AI can be a game-changer, sparking imagination and awakening a pioneering spirit within nonprofits. Instead of viewing technology adoption as a resource-intensive endeavor, AI presents an opportunity for nonprofits to leverage advanced tools without compromising their primary mission of service delivery. It becomes a force multiplier, allowing nonprofits to achieve more with their existing resources and empowering them to tackle challenges that were once deemed insurmountable.

Our ultimate goal is to inspire a shift in perspective—a realization that AI is not just a technological innovation but a partner in advancing social impact. By fostering a culture of curiosity and embracing the transformative potential of AI, nonprofits can unlock new possibilities, break free from the constraints of limited resources, and chart a course toward more effective and sustainable community service. The vision is one where AI becomes an enabler, empowering nonprofits to not only meet the demands of today but to pioneer innovative solutions that shape the landscape of tomorrow.

In navigating the intersection of AI and the Nonprofit sector, it's crucial to dispel any apprehensions and instead embrace this new technology as a catalyst for transformative change. The nonprofit sector should view AI not as a formidable challenge but as a powerful ally in fulfilling its mission to create healthier, more resilient, just, and equitable lives and communities.

By adopting and implementing AI, nonprofits can position themselves as early adopters, ready to leverage the full spectrum of benefits that this technology offers. The prospect of becoming pioneers in AI adoption holds the promise of expanding the sector's capacity to do good.

It's a call to action for the Nonprofit sector to be proactive, to embark on the journey of AI adoption at its dawn. This proactive stance is not just about embracing a new technological tool; it's about seizing a profound opportunity to bridge gaps and amplify the sector's impact. History will judge whether the sector embraced this pivotal moment, recognizing the tremendous opportunity that AI presented for organizational growth, innovation, and improved service delivery.

For a sector that has accomplished so much with limited resources over an extended period, AI emerges as a timely and deserving ally. The capabilities of AI as a Decision Support Tool align seamlessly with the sector's ethos of doing more with less. The journey into the realm of AI is not just a technological progression; it's a commitment to continuous improvement, resilience, and a deeper fulfillment of the sector's mission.

AI and Job Worries

"Are we going to lose jobs because of AI?" is a question that echoes in the corridors of businesses, nonprofits, and even our daily conversations. It's true that AI and technological advancements are reshaping the landscape of employment, but this transformation isn't necessarily a harbinger of job loss. Instead, it's a sign of change, a continuation of the evolution that work has undergone for centuries.

Let's take a step back and consider the industrial revolution, a period marked by a seismic shift in manufacturing processes. People feared the worst, envisioning a world where machines usurped human roles, leaving widespread unemployment in their wake. While it's true that some jobs became obsolete, an array of new opportunities sprang up. Individuals transitioned from agrarian work to roles in burgeoning factories, and as time progressed, they found places in sectors that didn't exist before, like information technology and digital communications.

Fast forward to the Internet era, another milestone in the history of human progress. The advent of the Internet revolutionized the way we live and work, birthing entirely new industries and job roles. Yes, some positions were phased out as automation and online platforms became more prevalent, but simultaneously, new avenues opened up. Web designers, digital marketers, and cybersecurity specialists are just a few examples of roles that emerged in the wake of the Internet revolution.

Now, as we stand on the brink of the AI evolution, it's natural to feel a sense of déjà vu. AI is transforming industries, automating tasks, and making some jobs redundant. However, it's also paving the way for new types of employment, roles that require a new set of skills and expertise. AI is not just about robots and algorithms; it's about how we harness this technology to enhance our capabilities and explore new frontiers.

In the nonprofit sector, for instance, AI could automate routine administrative tasks, freeing up staff to focus on strategy and human-centric roles that AI can't replicate, like community engagement and personalized support. Similarly, in health care, while AI might streamline data processing and diagnostic procedures, the need for compassionate care, empathy, and human judgment remains paramount—qualities that AI cannot emulate.

The key to navigating this shift is adaptability. Just as our predecessors adapted to the changes brought by the industrial revolution and the Internet, we too can learn to coexist with AI. This means embracing lifelong learning, staying abreast of new developments, and being willing to acquire new skills that complement the capabilities of AI.

Moreover, as AI takes over more routine and repetitive tasks, it presents us with an opportunity to redefine what work means to us. It encourages a shift toward more creative, strategic, and interpersonal roles, allowing individuals to explore careers that are more aligned with their passions and interests.

In conclusion, while AI and technological advancements may phase out certain jobs, they also lay the groundwork for new opportunities. Our civilization has always found a way to adapt and thrive amidst change, and the rise of AI is no exception. The future of work isn't about competing with machines; it's about leveraging AI to enhance our innate human qualities and exploring new realms of possibility. So, the mantra in this era of AI isn't to be scared but to be prepared, ready to embrace the changes and opportunities that this technological revolution brings.

AI's Role in Decision Making

When contemplating the role of AI in decision making, it's crucial to differentiate between AI as a decision-maker and decision-support tool. The distinction lies in the fact that while AI can process data and provide recommendations, the ultimate decision-making power and responsibility remain with humans.

AI is best conceptualized as a sophisticated decision support system. It excels at sifting through large volumes of data, identifying patterns, and providing actionable insights, which can be invaluable in aiding human decision-making processes. However, it's important to recognize that AI does not replace human judgment but rather augments it.

A relatable example of this concept is the use of car navigation systems. These systems, powered by AI, have gradually earned our trust by efficiently calculating routes, estimating travel times, and suggesting alternative paths to avoid traffic congestion. They demonstrate the ability of AI to assist in decision making by providing us with information that we might not have readily available or might take a considerable amount of time to gather.

Just like car navigation systems, AI in broader contexts should be approached with a balance of trust and caution. Navigation systems, for all their utility, occasionally make mistakes—they might suggest a longer route, misinterpret traffic conditions, or not be updated with the latest road changes. These errors remind us that while AI systems can be highly reliable, they are not infallible. Similarly, AI applications in other areas, whether in health care, finance, or customer service, should be used with an understanding of their limitations.

This analogy brings us back to the fundamental truth: just as we are still the drivers in our cars, ultimately making the final decisions based on the information provided by the navigation system, in all AI applications, humans are still the decision makers. We must interpret AI's recommendations within the broader context, considering factors that the AI may not be programmed to understand or assess.

AI should be seen as a valuable tool in the decision-making arsenal, not the sole decision maker. Its role as a decision support system is to enhance human capabilities, not to replace them. This perspective ensures that we leverage AI's strengths—its speed, efficiency, and data-processing capabilities—while maintaining human oversight, judgment, and accountability, which are essential in navigating the complexities of real-world decisions.

AI: Enhancing, Not Replacing, Human Decisions

When pondering the question, "Will AI take over our decision-making?" it's crucial to grasp that AI is fundamentally a decision support tool, not a decision maker in itself. This distinction underscores that humans remain firmly at the helm of critical decision-making processes, steering the course of actions based on AI-generated insights and recommendations.

AI's role is to sift through vast amounts of data, identify patterns, and present options with potential outcomes, thereby enhancing the quality of decisions by providing comprehensive, data-driven insights that humans might overlook. For instance, in the health care sector, AI can analyze patient data to suggest potential diagnosis or treatment plans, but the final call on patient care rests with medical professionals who consider a range of factors beyond what AI can compute.

The relationship between humans and AI in decision making is akin to a seasoned pilot navigating an aircraft with advanced avionics. While the technology provides valuable information and recommendations, the pilot makes the ultimate decisions, especially in critical situations, leveraging their experience, judgment, and understanding of the unique context.

As we grow accustomed to AI's capabilities and reliability, our trust in its recommendations will likely increase, allowing AI to take on more complex tasks and provide more sophisticated decision support. However, this doesn't equate to AI taking over decision making. Instead, it signifies a collaborative synergy where AI enhances human decision making, ensuring that decisions are informed by a blend of human insight and AI-generated data.

While AI will become increasingly integral in the decision-making landscape, offering insights that can transform how we analyze information and options, humans will always be the ultimate decision makers. This balance ensures that decisions remain grounded in human experience, empathy, and ethical considerations, with AI serving as a powerful tool to inform and support these decisions rather than replace them.

Authenticating AI: Humanity's Challenge

As we navigate the burgeoning landscape of AI, one of the emerging challenges we face is understanding the authenticity of AI-generated content. In the near future, distinguishing between a message crafted by AI and one composed by a human might become increasingly difficult. This challenge extends beyond text-based interactions to phone conversations and virtual meetings, where AI's ability to mimic human speech and responses can blur the lines of authenticity.

The integration of AI into our communication systems represents a new frontier for humanity, one that necessitates the development of new frameworks and standards to ensure transparency and trust. As we stand on the cusp of this technological evolution, it's comforting to know that researchers and institutions are already delving into this critical issue, working to establish standards and procedures to verify the authenticity of AI-generated content.

In any technological advancement, there are risks of misuse. Just as there will be AI used for beneficial purposes, there will inevitably be "bad" AI—systems designed with malicious intent or used unethically. This duality mirrors the broader human experience where innovation can be a double-edged sword, capable of both immense good and potential harm.

However, history shows us that humanity has a remarkable capacity to adapt and innovate in the face of new challenges. Just as we have developed systems to ensure the authenticity and security of digital transactions or the credibility of information online, we will develop methodologies to discern AI-generated content and interactions. These systems will evolve, becoming more sophisticated as AI itself advances.

While the journey ahead may be fraught with challenges, the collective ingenuity and ethical commitment of the global community will guide us toward solutions. We will establish protocols and standards that safeguard authenticity and trust in an AI-integrated world. The path forward is not just about technological innovation but also about shaping a framework where technology serves humanity's best interests, enhancing our lives while maintaining the core values of authenticity and integrity that define our human interactions.

Where to Start

Where to start in integrating AI into your nonprofit organization? You've already taken the first, crucial step by engaging with this book, broadening your understanding of AI's potential and its applicability within the nonprofit sector. Knowledge is the foundation upon which meaningful action is built, and by educating yourself, you're setting the stage for transformative change.

The next step is a thorough analysis of the AI tools available and an in-depth review of your organization's processes. This involves identifying areas within your operations where AI can have the most significant impact, whether it's streamlining administrative tasks, enhancing donor engagement, optimizing resource allocation, or improving service delivery. Understanding where your needs and the capabilities of AI intersect is key to identifying the most beneficial applications for your organization.

But knowledge and analysis will only take you so far. The crucial phase is the leap from theory to practice—the courageous step of implementing AI within your organization. This might seem daunting, but remember, embracing AI doesn't have to be an all-or-nothing proposition. Start small, with pilot projects or specific tasks where AI can be easily integrated and where results can be quickly observed. This gradual approach not only mitigates risk but also allows your team to adapt to and learn from each AI implementation, building confidence and expertise.

Embracing AI is a journey of continuous learning and adaptation. As your organization grows more accustomed to AI's capabilities and integrates these tools into various facets of operation, you'll discover new opportunities for application and improvement. Remember, the objective is not just to incorporate new technology but to harness it in a way that amplifies your mission and expands your impact.

The path forward begins with the knowledge you've gained, followed by a strategic analysis of where AI can enhance your operations, culminating in the bold step of implementation. By following this roadmap, you're not just adopting new technology; you're positioning your nonprofit at the forefront of innovation, ready to leverage the immense potential of AI to drive your mission forward.

Key Takeaway: AI Empowers Nonprofits

As we close this exploration into the world of AI for nonprofits, it's vital to address a common sentiment that often accompanies discussions about AI: fear. The rapid advancements in AI technology can seem daunting, and the prospect of integrating AI into the core functions of a nonprofit might feel overwhelming. However, the key to harnessing the power of AI is not fear but preparation.

Our motto "Don't be scared, be prepared" encapsulates the proactive stance nonprofits should adopt toward AI integration. Preparation means understanding the potential of AI to transform your organization's impact, operational efficiency, and engagement strategies. It involves educating your team about AI, demystifying its capabilities, and dispelling myths about its complexity or inaccessibility.

Being prepared also entails developing a strategic approach to AI adoption, which begins with identifying the areas within your organization where AI can have the most significant impact. It's about setting clear goals, whether that's improving donor engagement, enhancing program delivery, or boosting internal processes.

Moreover, preparation involves embracing a culture of learning and adaptability. As AI continues to evolve, so too should your organization's approach to leveraging it. This might mean ongoing training for staff, staying informed about new AI developments, and being open to adjusting your strategies as you learn what works best for your mission.

In embracing AI, it's crucial to partner with AI experts or leverage resources and networks that can provide guidance and support. This collaborative approach not only eases the transition into AI adoption but also ensures that your organization is using AI ethically and effectively, aligning with your core values and mission.

Let the Nonprofit sector boldly embark on this transformative journey. Let the ethos of early adoption and innovative spirit guide organizations in harnessing the potential of AI for the greater good. The sector has laid a foundation of resilience and impact with its tireless efforts, and now, with AI as a strategic partner, there's an opportunity to amplify its influence and contribute to a future where positive change is not just a goal but a reality. The dawn of AI marks the beginning of a new era for the Nonprofit sector—one where technology becomes an enabler of lasting and meaningful social impact.

So, as you stand at the frontier of AI in the nonprofit sector, remember that the future is not something to be feared but prepared for. With a thoughtful, strategic approach to AI, your organization can not only adapt to the future but actively shape it, enhancing your impact and expanding your reach in the communities you serve. Don't be scared; be prepared to embrace AI as a powerful ally in your mission to create positive change.

Notes

Chapter 1

1. Martin (2019).

Chapter 2

1. Woolliams (2016).

Chapter 3

1. Daum (2016).

Chapter 4

1. Warner (2018).

Chapter 5

1. Washington University in St.Louis Technology and Leadership Center (n.d.).

Chapter 6

1. Sayegh (2021).

Chapter 7

1. Zaslofsky (2012).

Chapter 8

1. Benjamin Franklin Quotes (n.d.).

Chapter 9

1. ProjectSkillsMentor.com (n.d.).

Chapter 10

1. Kenny (2020).

Chapter 11

1. Taylor (1919).

Chapter 12

1. Lavinsky (n.d.).

References

Benjamin Franklin Quotes." n.d. Goodreads.com.

Daum, K. 2016. "37 Quotes From Thomas Edison That Will Inspire Success." Inc.com.

How Do You Define Leadership?" n.d. Washington University in St. Louis Technology and Leadership Center, TLcenter.wustl.edu.

How to Build Your Personal Authority." n.d. ProjectSkillsMentor.com.

Kenny, C. 2020. "The Single Biggest Problem in Communication Is the Illusion That it Has Taken Place." IrishTimes.com.

Lavinsky, D. n.d. "The Two Most Important Quotes in Business." growthink.com.

Martin, N. 2019. "13 Best Quotes About the Future Of Artificial Intelligence." *Forbes.*

Sayegh, E. 2021. "Strategy vs. Tactics: Two Sides of a Difficult Coin." LawJournalNewsletters.com.

Taylor, F.W. 1919.In *The Principles of Scientific Management.* Harper and Brothers Publishers, New York and London.

Warner, J. 2018. "I am not Against Inspiring Words." InsideHigherEd.com.

Woolliams, R. 2016. "Stephen Hawking: AI Could Be Human History's Greatest Disaster—But There Is an Alternative." AIBusiness.com.

Zaslofsky, J. 2012. "A Statement to Reframe Everything? The Defining Factor Is Never Resources, It's Resourcefulness." joelzaslofsky.com.

About the Authors

Dr. Daniel O. Livvarcin is a renowned expert in the nonprofit sector and founder of Vectors Group, specializing in strategic management, risk evaluation, and AI integration. A prolific author and part-time professor, he passionately advocates for social equity and empowers organizations with innovative AI-driven frameworks and dedicated leadership.

Yacouba Traoré is an experienced executive director in the nonprofit sector, skilled in management, fundraising, coaching, and community engagement. He excels at leading organizations to achieve impactful outcomes through strategic direction and fostering community development, making him a respected and accomplished leader in the industry.

Index

OTHER TITLES IN THE HUMAN RESOURCE MANAGEMENT AND ORGANIZATIONAL BEHAVIOR COLLECTION

Michael J. Provitera and Michael Edmondson, Editors

- *Ignite All* by The Fusion Team
- *(Re)Value* by Adam Wallace and Adam Wallace
- *Dysfunctional Organizations* by David D. Van Fleet
- *The Negotiation Edge* by Michael Saksa
- *Applied Leadership* by Sam Altawil
- *Forging Dynasty Businesses* by Chuck Violand
- *How the Harvard Business School Changed the Way We View Organizations* by Jay W. Lorsch
- *Managing Millennials* by Jacqueline Cripps
- *Personal Effectiveness* by Lucia Strazzeri
- *Catalyzing Transformation* by Sandra Waddock
- *Critical Leadership and Management Tools for Contemporary Organizations* by Tony Miller
- *Leading From the Top* by Dennis M. Powell
- *Warp Speed Habits* by Marco Neves
- *I Don't Understand* by Buki Mosaku
- *Nurturing Equanimity* by Michael Edmondson

Concise and Applied Business Books

The Collection listed above is one of 30 business subject collections that Business Expert Press has grown to make BEP a premiere publisher of print and digital books. Our concise and applied books are for...

- Professionals and Practitioners
- Faculty who adopt our books for courses
- Librarians who know that BEP's Digital Libraries are a unique way to offer students ebooks to download, not restricted with any digital rights management
- Executive Training Course Leaders
- Business Seminar Organizers

Business Expert Press books are for anyone who needs to dig deeper on business ideas, goals, and solutions to everyday problems. Whether one print book, one ebook, or buying a digital library of 110 ebooks, we remain the affordable and smart way to be business smart. For more information, please visit www.businessexpertpress.com, or contact sales@businessexpertpress.com.

www.ingramcontent.com/pod-product-compliance
Lightning Source LLC
Chambersburg PA
CBHW061215220326
41599CB00025B/4650